FAVOURITE
FAMILY
Poetry

167 - Neruda, war - web?

165 - Death

162 - Marlowe

155 - Gremenbutes

135 - Bronte

134 - Auden

130 - Xmas

123 - The garden

118 - Lorca

115 - Herrick

FAVOURITE
FAMILY
Poetry

Foreword by
Felicity Kendal

MICHAEL JOSEPH
London

MICHAEL JOSEPH LTD

Published by the Penguin Group
27 Wrights Lane, London W8 5TZ
Viking Penguin Inc., 375 Hudson Street, New York, New York 10014, USA
Penguin Books Australia Ltd, Ringwood, Victoria, Australia
Penguin Books Canada Ltd, 10 Alcorn Avenue, Toronto, Ontario, Canada M4V 3B2
Penguin Books (NZ) Ltd, 182–190 Wairau Road, Auckland 10, New Zealand

Penguin Books Ltd, Registered Offices: Harmondsworth, Middlesex, England

First published 1995

This collection copyright © Michael Joseph 1995
Foreword copyright © Felicity Kendal 1995
Copyright of individual poems as in the acknowledgements
Illustrations copyright © Peter McClure 1995

Typeset by Datix International Limited, Bungay, Suffolk
Printed in England by Clays Ltd, St Ives plc
Filmset in 11/12.5 pt Monophoto Bembo

A CIP catalogue record for this book is available
from the British Library

ISBN 0 7181 3978 X

The moral right of the author has been asserted

9/10/95

All royalties from this book are to be donated to:

LEUKAEMIA RESEARCH FUND
43 Great Ormond Street, London WC1N 3JJ
Telephone: 0171-405 0101

Registered Charity 216032

Contents

[5]

Note on the Selection of Poems

~~~~~~~~~~~~~~~~~~~~~~~~~~~~~~~~~~~~~~

EACH contributor was invited to choose their ten favourite poems. The poems selected between them were ranked by the following points system.

Where the poems were listed in order of preference, a number ten was given 11 points, a number nine 12 points, a number eight 13 points and so on, up to 19 points for a number two. Each number one poem was given 21 points. Where the contributors chose not to rank their top ten in order, the total number of points available, 156, was divided by ten and each poem was given 15.6 points.

The 100 highest-scoring poems were printed in *The Family Poetry Book*, published in 1990. The aim of this new volume was to print the next 100 most popular poems, ranked by the same points system. However, because 64 poems contested equally for the last 25 places and there was only space to include 100 poems, each poet has been limited to no more than three entries. Using this system, the poems are listed in order of popularity and alphabetically within each ranking.

A full list of each contributor's choice of poems appears on pages pp. 183–203.

Foreword

In my foreword to *The Family Poetry Book*, to which *Favourite Family Poetry* is a companion, I said I hoped that 'it will establish itself as a favourite anthology to be picked up by those who like to come across an old friend, well remembered or half-forgotten, or equally to make a new one.'

How I wish that all my hopes could be as successfully realized. That earlier anthology is now in its seventh impression. I believe that this second book is going to be a worthy companion to the first. It's a wonderful collection of poetry.

We have returned to the same well and drawn another volume from the poems which were originally submitted by fifty-two well-known people. So, if you're like me the 'Who chose what?' element will once more give extra pleasure to dipping into these pages.

Last time those who were asked to nominate their top ten came up with about four hundred poems and only a quarter of those found room in the book. For a start, half of mine did not get in!

There must have been many readers who looked at the first book with disbelief and outrage. 'What, no A. A. Milne? No Rossetti? How can they leave out 'The Dong with a Luminous Nose'?

Have patience. Look again. I did and – what did I find? All my missing five, tucked in among some of the poems that might have been on my own list if I had been allowed a top twenty – not to mention some which were new to me and are now making their way into the company of my favourites.

Such are the pleasures waiting here for all who love poetry – and also perhaps for some of the youngest members of the family who are about to discover that they love poetry. *They* will find that a life which includes both Keats and Carroll is a greater joy than a life which knows only one or the other.

The principle on which this collection has been assembled ensures just such a jostling together and I'm sure that's why these personal favourites will make another favourite anthology.

As before, the Leukemia Research Fund will benefit from this book, and I'm very pleased to applaud it as the right book for the right occasion. It is surely in our poetry that we can find all the journeys of the heart through joy and loss, hope and fulfilment and love.

So, on behalf of the Fund, let me thank the publishers, the contributors and, above all, the readers. And if you have already looked at the table of Contents and cried out 'What?! No —?', have patience. This well may not be dry.

Felicity Kendal, CBE

1 June 1995

THE POEMS

Naming of Parts

ॐ

TODAY we have naming of parts. Yesterday,
We had daily cleaning. And tomorrow morning,
We shall have what to do after firing. But today,
Today we have naming of parts. Japonica
Glistens like coral in all of the neighbouring gardens,
        And today we have naming of parts.

This is the lower sling swivel. And this
Is the upper sling swivel, whose use you will see,
When you are given your slings. And this is the piling swivel,
Which in your case you have not got. The branches
Hold in the gardens their silent, eloquent gestures,
        Which in our case we have not got.

This is the safety-catch, which is always released
With an easy flick of the thumb. And please do not let me
See anyone using his finger. You can do it quite easy
If you have any strength in your thumb. The blossoms
Are fragile and motionless, never letting anyone see
        Any of them using their finger.

And this you can see is the bolt. The purpose of this
Is to open the breech, as you see. We can slide it
Rapidly backwards and forwards: we call this
Easing the spring. And rapidly backwards and forwards
The early bees are assaulting and fumbling the flowers:
        They call it easing the Spring.

They call it easing the Spring: it is perfectly easy
If you have any strength in your thumb: like the bolt,
And the breech, and the cocking-piece, and the point of balance,
Which in our case we have not got; and the almond-blossom
Silent in all of the gardens and the bees going backwards and forwards,
        For today we have naming of parts.

HENRY REED

[15]

Matilda

WHO TOLD LIES, AND WAS BURNED TO DEATH

MATILDA told such Dreadful Lies,
It made one Gasp and Stretch one's Eyes;
Her Aunt, who, from her Earliest Youth,
Had kept a Strict Regard for Truth,
Attempted to Believe Matilda:
The effort very nearly killed her,
And would have done so, had not She
Discovered this Infirmity.
For once, towards the Close of Day,
Matilda, growing tired of play,
And finding she was left alone,
Went tiptoe to the Telephone
And summoned the Immediate Aid
Of London's Noble Fire-Brigade.
Within an hour the Gallant Band
Were pouring in on every hand,
From Putney, Hackney Downs, and Bow.
With Courage high and Hearts a-glow,
They galloped, roaring through the Town,
'Matilda's House is Burning Down!'
Inspired by British Cheers and Loud
Proceeding from the Frenzied Crowd,
They ran their ladders through a score
Of windows on the Ball Room Floor;
And took Peculiar Pains to Souse
The Pictures up and down the House,
Until Matilda's Aunt succeeded
In showing them they were not needed;
And even then she had to pay
To get the Men to go away!

It happened that a few Weeks later
Her Aunt was off to the Theatre
To see that Interesting Play
The Second Mrs Tanqueray.
She had refused to take her Niece
To hear this Entertaining Piece:
A Deprivation Just and Wise
To Punish her for Telling Lies.
That Night a Fire *did* break out —
You should have heard Matilda Shout!
You should have heard her Scream and Bawl,
And throw the window up and call
To People passing in the Street —
(The rapidly increasing Heat
Encouraging her to obtain
Their confidence) — but all in vain!
For every time She shouted 'Fire!'
They only answered 'Little Liar!'
And therefore when her Aunt returned,
Matilda, and the House, were Burned.

HILAIRE BELLOC

Sunlight

THERE was a sunlit absence.
The helmeted pump in the yard
heated its iron,
water honeyed

in the slung bucket
and the sun stood
like a griddle cooling
against the wall

of each long afternoon.
So, her hands scuffled
over the bakeboard,
the reddening stove

sent its plaque of heat
against her where she stood
in a floury apron
by the window.

Now she dusts the board
with a goose's wing,
now sits, broad-lapped,
with whitened nails

and measling shins:
here is a space
again, the scone rising
to the tick of two clocks.

And here is love
like a tinsmith's scoop
sunk past its gleam
in the meal-bin.

from *Mossbawn: Two Poems in Dedication*
for Mary Heaney
SEAMUS HEANEY

'When I was one-and-twenty'

WHEN I was one-and-twenty
   I heard a wise man say,
'Give crowns and pounds and guineas
   But not your heart away;
Give pearls away and rubies
   But keep your fancy free.'
But I was one-and-twenty,
   No use to talk to me.

When I was one-and-twenty
   I heard him say again,
'The heart out of the bosom
   Was never given in vain;
'Tis paid with sighs a plenty
   And sold for endless rue.'
And I am two-and-twenty,
   And oh, 'tis true, 'tis true.

from *A Shropshire Lad*
A.E. HOUSMAN

The Child Who was Shot Dead by Soldiers at Nyanga

THE child is not dead
the child lifts his fists against his mother
who shouts Afrika! shouts the breath
of freedom and the veld
in the locations of the cordoned heart

The child lifts his fists against his father
in the march of the generations
who are shouting Afrika! shout the breath
of righteousness and blood
in the streets of his embattled pride

The child is not dead
not at Langa nor at Nyanga
nor at Orlando nor at Sharpeville
nor at the police post in Philippi
where he lies with a bullet through his brain

The child is the dark shadow of the soldiers
on guard with their rifles, saracens and batons
the child is present at all assemblies and law-giving
the child peers through the windows of houses and into the hearts of
    mothers
this child who wanted only to play in the sun at Nyanga is
    everywhere
the child grown to a man treks on through all Africa
the child grown into a giant journeys over the whole world

Without a pass

INGRID JONKER

Ode on Melancholy

No, no! go not to Lethe, neither twist
　　Wolf's-bane, tight-rooted, for its poisonous wine;
Nor suffer thy pale forehead to be kiss'd
　　By nightshade, ruby grape of Proserpine;
Make not your rosary of yew-berries,
　　Nor let the beetle, nor the death-moth be
　　　　Your mournful Psyche, nor the downy owl
A partner in your sorrow's mysteries;
　　For shade to shade will come too drowsily,
　　　　And drown the wakeful anguish of the soul.

But when the melancholy fit shall fall
　　Sudden from heaven like a weeping cloud,
That fosters the droop-headed flowers all,
　　And hides the green hill in an April shroud;
Then glut thy sorrow on a morning rose,
　　Or on the rainbow of the salt sand-wave,
　　　　Or on the wealth of globèd peonies;
Or if thy mistress some rich anger shows,
　　Emprison her soft hand, and let her rave,
　　　　And feed deep, deep upon her peerless eyes.

She dwells with Beauty – Beauty that must die;
　　And Joy, whose hand is ever at his lips
Bidding adieu; and aching Pleasure nigh,
　　Turning to poison while the bee-mouth sips:
Ay, in the very temple of Delight
　　Veil'd Melancholy has her sovran shrine,
　　　　Though seen of none save him whose strenuous tongue
　　Can burst Joy's grape against his palate fine:
His soul shall taste the sadness of her might,
　　And be among her cloudy trophies hung.

JOHN KEATS

[21]

Show Saturday

GREY day for the Show, but cars jam the narrow lanes.
Inside, on the field, judging has started: dogs
(Set their legs back, hold out their tails) and ponies (manes
Repeatedly smoothed, to calm heads); over there, sheep
(Cheviot and Blackface); by the hedge, squealing logs
(Chain Saw Competition). Each has its own keen crowd.
In the main arena, more judges meet by a jeep:
The jumping's on next. Announcements, splutteringly loud,

Clash with the quack of a man with pound notes round his hat
And a lit-up board. There's more than just animals:
Bead-stalls, balloon-men, a Bank; a beer-marquee that
Half-screens a canvas Gents; a tent selling tweed,
And another, jackets. Folks sit about on bales
Like great straw dice. For each scene is linked by spaces
Not given to anything much, where kids scrap, freed,
While their owners stare different ways with incurious faces.

The wrestling starts, late; a wide ring of people; then cars;
Then trees; then pale sky. Two young men in acrobats' tights
And embroidered trunks hug each other; rock over the grass,
Stiff-legged, in a two-man scrum. One falls: they shake hands.
Two more start, one grey-haired: he wins, though. They're not so
        much fights
As long immobile strainings that end in unbalance
With one on his back, unharmed, while the other stands
Smoothing his hair. But there are other talents –

The long high tent of growing and making, wired-off
Wood tables past which crowds shuffle, eyeing the scrubbed spaced
Extrusions of earth: blanch leeks like church candles, six pods of
Broad beans (one split open), dark shining-leafed cabbages – rows
Of single supreme versions, followed (on laced
        Paper mats) by dairy and kitchen; four brown eggs, four white eggs,
Four plain scones, four dropped scones, pure excellences that enclose
A recession of skills. And, after them, lambing-sticks, rugs,

Needlework, knitted caps, baskets, all worthy, all well done,
But less than the honeycombs. Outside, the jumping's over.
The young ones thunder their ponies in competition
Twice round the ring; then trick races, Musical Stalls,
Sliding off, riding bareback, the ponies dragged to and fro for
Bewildering requirements, not minding. But now, in the background,
Like shifting scenery, horse-boxes move; each crawls
Towards the stock entrance, tilting and swaying, bound

For far-off farms. The pound-note man decamps.
The car park has thinned. They're loading jumps on a truck.
Back now to private addresses, gates and lamps
In high stone one-street villages, empty at dusk,
And side roads of small towns (sports finals stuck
In front doors, allotments reaching down to the railway);
Back now to autumn, leaving the ended husk
Of summer that brought them here for Show Saturday –

The men with hunters, dog-breeding wool-defined women,
Children all saddle-swank, mugfaced middleaged wives
Glaring at jellies, husbands on leave from the garden
Watchful as weasels, car-tuning curt-haired sons –
Back now, all of them, to their local lives:
To names on vans, and business calendars
Hung up in kitchens; back to loud occasions
In the Corn Exchange, to market days in bars,
To winter coming, as the dismantled Show
Itself dies back into the area of work.
Let it stay hidden there like strength, below
Sale-bills and swindling; something people do,
Not noticing how time's rolling smithy-smoke
Shadows much greater gestures; something they share
That breaks ancestrally each year into
Regenerate union. Let it always be there.

PHILIP LARKIN

The Sunlight on the Garden

THE sunlight on the garden
Hardens and grows cold,
We cannot cage the minute
Within its nets of gold,
When all is told
We cannot beg for pardon.

Our freedom as free lances
Advances towards its end;
The earth compels, upon it
Sonnets and birds descend;
And soon, my friend,
We shall have no time for dances.

The sky was good for flying
Defying the church bells
And every evil iron
Siren and what it tells:
The earth compels,
We are dying, Egypt, dying

And not expecting pardon,
Hardened in heart anew,
But glad to have sat under
Thunder and rain with you,
And grateful too
For sunlight on the garden.

LOUIS MACNEICE

Halfway Down

ನಲ

HALFWAY down the stairs
Is a stair
Where I sit.
There isn't any
Other stair
Quite like
It.
I'm not at the bottom,
I'm not at the top;
So this is the stair
Where
I always
Stop.

Halfway up the stairs
Isn't up,
And isn't down.
It isn't in the nursery,
It isn't in the town.
And all sorts of funny thoughts
Run round my head:
'It isn't really
Anywhere!
It's somewhere else
Instead!'

A. A. MILNE

Solitude

I HAVE a house where I go
   When there's too many people,
I have a house where I go
   Where no one can be;
I have a house where I go,
Where nobody ever says 'No'
Where no one says anything – so
   There is no one but me.

A. A. MILNE

Disabled

He sat in a wheeled chair, waiting for dark,
And shivered in his ghastly suit of grey,
Legless, sewn short at elbow. Through the park
Voices of boys rang saddening like a hymn,
Voices of play and pleasure after day,
Till gathering sleep had mothered them from him.

About this time Town used to swing so gay
When glow-lamps budded in the light blue trees,
And girls glanced lovelier as the air grew dim,
– In the old times, before he threw away his knees.
Now he will never feel again how slim
Girls' waists are, or how warm their subtle hands.
All of them touch him like some queer disease.

There was an artist silly for his face,
For it was younger than his youth, last year.
Now, he is old; his back will never brace;
He's lost his colour very far from here,
Poured it down shell-holes till the veins ran dry,
And half his lifetime lapsed in the hot race
And leap of purple spurted from his thigh.
One time he liked a bloodsmear down his leg,
After the matches, carried shoulder-high.
It was after football, when he'd drunk a peg,
He thought he'd better join. – He wonders why.
Someone had said he'd look a god in kilts,
That's why; and maybe, too, to please his Meg,
Aye, that was it, to please the giddy jilts
He asked to join. He didn't have to beg;
Smiling they wrote his lie: aged nineteen years.
Germans he scarcely thought of; all their guilt,
And Austria's, did not move him. And no fears
Of Fear came yet. He thought of jewelled hilts
For daggers in plaid socks; of smart salutes;
And care of arms; and leave; and pay arrears;

Esprit de corps; and hints for young recruits.
And soon, he was drafted out with drums and cheers.

Some cheered him home, but not as crowds cheer Goal.
Only a solemn man who brought him fruits
Thanked him; and then inquired about his soul.

Now, he will spend a few sick years in institutes,
And do what things the rules consider wise,
And take whatever pity they may dole.
Tonight he noticed how the women's eyes
Passed from him to the strong men that were whole.
How cold and late it is! Why don't they come
And put him into bed? Why don't they come?

WILFRED OWEN

Sonnet 66

ಎ೭

TIRED with all these, for restful death I cry,
As, to behold desert a beggar born,
And needy nothing trimm'd in jollity,
And purest faith unhappily forsworn,
And gilded honour shamefully misplaced,
And maiden virtue rudely strumpeted,
And right perfection wrongfully disgraced,
And strength by limping sway disabled,
And art made tongue-tied by authority,
And folly, doctor-like, controlling skill,
And simple truth miscall'd simplicity,
And captive good attending captain ill:
    Tired with all these, from these would I be gone,
    Save that, to die, I leave my love alone.

WILLIAM SHAKESPEARE

Ode to the West Wind

I

O WILD West Wind, thou breath of Autumn's being,
Thou, from whose unseen presence the leaves dead
Are driven, like ghosts from an enchanter fleeing,

Yellow, and black, and pale, and hectic red,
Pestilence-stricken multitudes: O thou,
Who chariotest to their dark wintry bed

The wingèd seeds, where they lie cold and low,
Each like a corpse within its grave, until
Thine azure sister of the Spring shall blow

Her clarion o'er the dreaming earth, and fill
(Driving sweet buds like flocks to feed in air)
With living hues and odours plain and hill:

Wild Spirit, which art moving everywhere;
Destroyer and preserver; hear, oh, hear!

II

Thou on whose stream, mid the steep sky's commotion,
Loose clouds like earth's decaying leaves are shed,
Shook from the tangled boughs of Heaven and Ocean,

Angels of rain and lighting: there are spread
On the blue surface of thine airy surge,
Like the bright hair uplifted from the head

Of some fierce Maenad, even from the dim verge
Of the horizon to the zenith's height,
The locks of the approaching storm. Thou dirge

Of the dying year, to which this closing night
Will be the dome of a vast sepulchre,
Vaulted with all thy congregated might

Of vapours, from whose solid atmosphere
Black rain, and fire, and hail will burst: oh, hear!

III

Thou who didst waken from his summer dreams
The blue Mediterranean, where he lay,
Lulled by the coil of his crystàlline streams,

Beside a pumice isle in Baiae's bay,
And saw in sleep old palaces and towers
Quivering within the wave's intenser day,

All overgrown with azure moss and flowers
So sweet, the sense faints picturing them! Thou
For whose path the Atlantic's level powers

Cleave themselves into chasms, while far below
The sea-blooms and the oozy woods which wear
The sapless foliage of the ocean, know

Thy voice, and suddenly grow grey with fear,
And tremble and despoil themselves: oh, hear!

IV

If I were a dead leaf thou mightest bear;
If I were a swift cloud to fly with thee;
A wave to pant beneath thy power, and share

The impulse of thy strength, only less free
Than thou, O uncontrollable! If even
I were as in my boyhood, and could be

The comrade of thy wanderings over Heaven,
As then, when to outstrip thy skiey speed
Scarce seemed a vision; I would ne'er have striven

As thus with thee in prayer in my sore need.
Oh, lift me as a wave, a leaf, a cloud!
I fall upon the thorns of life! I bleed!

A heavy weight of hours has chained and bowed
One too like thee: tameless, and swift, and proud.

V

Make me thy lyre, even as the forest is:
What if my leaves are falling like its own!
The tumult of thy mighty harmonies

Will take from both a deep, autumnal tone,
Sweet though in sadness. Be thou, Spirit fierce,
My spirit! Be thou me, impetuous one!

Drive my dead thoughts over the universe
Like withered leaves to quicken a new birth!
And, by the incantation of this verse,

Scatter, as from an unextinguished hearth
Ashes and sparks, my words among mankind!
Be through my lips to unawakened earth

The trumpet of a prophecy! O, Wind,
If Winter comes, can Spring be far behind?

PERCY BYSSHE SHELLEY

Chorus from 'Atalanta'

WHEN the hounds of spring are on winter's traces,
   The mother of months in meadow or plain
Fills the shadows and windy places
   With lisp of leaves and ripple of rain;
And the brown bright nightingale amorous
Is half assuaged for Itylus,
For the Thracian ships and the foreign faces,
   The tongueless vigil, and all the pain.

Come with bows bent and with emptying of quivers,
   Maiden most perfect, lady of light,
With a noise of winds and many rivers,
   With a clamour of waters, and with might;
Bind on thy sandals, O thou most fleet,
Over the splendour and speed of thy feet;
For the faint east quickens, the wan west shivers,
   Round the feet of the day and the feet of the night.

Where shall we find her, how shall we sing to her,
   Fold our hands round her knees, and cling?
O that man's heart were as fire and could spring to her,
   Fire, or the strength of the streams that spring!
For the stars and the winds are unto her
As raiment, as songs of the harp-player;
For the risen stars and the fallen cling to her,
   And the southwest-wind and the west-wind sing.

For winter's rains and ruins are over,
   And all the season of snows and sins;
The days dividing lover and lover,
   The light that loses, the night that wins;
And time remember'd is grief forgotten,
And frosts are slain and flowers begotten,
And in green underwood and cover
   Blossom by blossom the spring begins.

The full streams feed on flower of rushes,
    Ripe grasses trammel a travelling foot,
The faint fresh flame of the young year flushes
    From leaf to flower and flower to fruit;
And fruit and leaf are as gold and fire,
And the oat is heard above the lyre,
And the hoofèd heel of a satyr crushes
    The chestnut-husk at the chestnut-root.

And Pan by noon and Bacchus by night,
    Fleeter of foot than the fleet-foot kid,
Follows with dancing and fills with delight
    The Maenad and the Bassarid;
And soft as lips that laugh and hide
The laughing leaves of the trees divide,
And screen from seeing and leave in sight
    The god pursuing, the maiden hid.

The ivy falls with the Bacchanal's hair
    Over her eyebrows hiding her eyes;
The wild vine slipping down leaves bare
    Her bright breast shortening into sighs;
The wild vine slips with the weight of its leaves,
But the berried ivy catches and cleaves
To the limbs that glitter, the feet that scare
    The wolf that follows, the fawn that flies.

ALGERNON CHARLES SWINBURNE

from *A Dream in the Luxembourg*

Si vis amari, ama

1

THERE are plenty of people to despise the dreamer of day-dreams,
And I've a friend, a learned friend with a wistful smile,
Who calls it a disease we inherit from Rousseau,
But I doubt if the learned friend has ever been really in love –
Sleepless, eatless, let Rome in Tiber melt love.
But never mind him, let me tell you my day-dream,
For who can be in love, in Paris, in June,
And the lady of his thoughts in another country,
Without day-dreaming under the trees in the Luxembourg?

Now I am so much moved as I write this
That my hand shakes with excitement,
And there is so much to say
I scarcely know where and how to begin;
So hard is it to be truly Reasonable
When you are a little crazy with a Romantick love.

2

When I least expected it, the miracle happened,
For I saw a wood-nymph visibly seated before me
In the shape of a girl . . .
And Love pierced me to the heart so that the wound still throbs.
But I mean it – that Eros of the Euripidean chorus,
That Amor you may read of in Catullus,
Had me in His power – that same Amor Peire Vidal saw
One spring morning riding through the fields of Provence –
And it is quite true, as the Ancients and the Romance poets knew,
That love is a sudden thing which stabs at the vitals
And leaves an ache like a wound in the left breast.
I was only near her for four days
And all that time my mind was in confusion,
For there were so many reasons why I should not love again,
And so many reasons why I should not love her.

[35]

So I fought against my love, trying to be 'honourable',
And I was so miserable and in such agony of mind
It was like the dark night of the spirit
Which the mystics know when their God abandons them.
But on the second day there came a moment when I ceased to
     struggle,
Let myself taste the happiness of being near her;
For a moment my eyes met hers, and for a moment
I gazed into the loveliest of human minds –
The water knew its God and blushed.
I was the water, and she was my God.
Then I saw that the Gods had brought me
A laughing tree-nymph, crisp-haired like the ilex,
With eyes that seem immortal.

I said to myself: This will cause me much agony,
For doubtless she will never love me –
What is one more lover to her
Who must have many lovers offering her devotion
And their peerless selves in exchange for her complaisance?
Doubtless she thinks me a lout or a fool
Because I am silent or stammer when she speaks to me.
But who shall strive against the Gods?

3

What is there in life that endures?
Why do we assume that love must last for ever?
Why can we not be wise like the Epicureans
Who thought not of possession but of enjoyment?
Is not a man a man, and a woman a woman?
If she loved me, should I mind that she has had lovers?
Are we Jews or Catholic bigots
Or – which is even worse – rich pious Methodists?
Did Epicurus love Leontion?
Did he not love Ternissa? Yes or No?
Was Lesbia so faithful to Catullus?
Well then? All we have's today.
Cras amet, if you can,
And if you really love once in a life,
Give thanks to all the Gods,
You'll not find love at every street-corner
Nor every drawing room either.

Yesterday I plucked out two grey hairs.
Memento mori. Yet a few more years,
And what remains of me and – hell! – of her?
Must fair women die?
I'll not believe it, Death is masculine.
Death, like a war-lord, wants more man-power,
And, by God, he gets it, I've seen him get it.

How many yellow dead men have I seen?
Carried how many stretchers?
Stood by how many graves – of young men, too?
Reported how many casualties?
But one gets used to it, quite used to it,
And it seems nothing for men to die,
Nothing for one to die oneself.
But for a fair woman to die,
And that a woman one loves or has loved –
No, it is incredible, they don't die,
They turn into the brightest flowers
Or become young graceful trees,
Or lovely white-winged sea-birds,
Or the lovelier fragile clouds
Poised like warm snow in the summer air.
Could not Alcestis and Admetus change their rôles?
After some happy weeks or months or years
What lover would refuse?
Of many murmured kisses give her the rich last,
Gaily take leave, and grasp the proffered hand
Of Hermes, Leader of the Dead,
Give her some twenty years you might have lived
A selfish, dwindling, middle-aged dull man,
And let her keep her youth,
And give her to a younger lover's arms,
Who, in his turn, shall give his life for hers!

I say she shall not die . . .

4

It was five on a sunny afternoon,
And I sat on one of those uncomfortable iron chairs
Under the trees of the Luxembourg,

Rather apart from the crowd,
So that the passing people seemed like trees moving,
And the children playing, like graceful forest animals;
In the distance I could see the wavering fountain jet,
Always rising and always falling in foamy parabolas
Like the path of a comet fixed in tremulous water.
And all this I am trying to tell you
Is the day-dream which suddenly came to me . . .

RICHARD ALDINGTON

Hunter Trials

It's awf'lly bad luck on Diana,
  Her ponies have swallowed their bits;
She fished down their throats with a spanner
  And frightened them all into fits.

So now she's attempting to borrow.
  Do lend her some bits, Mummy, *do*;
I'll lend her my own for tomorrow,
  But today *I*'ll be wanting them too.

Just look at Prunella on Guzzle,
  The wizardest pony on earth;
Why doesn't she slacken his muzzle
  And tighten the breech in his girth?

I say, Mummy, there's Mrs Geyser
  And doesn't she look pretty sick?
I bet it's because Mona Lisa
  Was hit on the hock with a brick.

Miss Blewitt says Monica threw it,
  But Monica says it was Joan,
And Joan's very thick with Miss Blewitt,
  So Monica's sulking alone.

And Margaret failed in her paces,
  Her withers got tied in a noose,
So her coronets caught in the traces
  And now all her fetlocks are loose.

Oh, it's me now. I'm terribly nervous.
  I wonder if Smudges will shy.
She's practically certain to swerve as
  Her Pelham is over one eye.

Oh wasn't it naughty of Smudges?
    Oh, Mummy, I'm sick with disgust.
She threw me in front of the Judges,
    And my silly old collarbone's bust.

JOHN BETJEMAN

The Busy Heart

Now that we've done our best and worst, and parted,
I would fill my mind with thoughts that will not rend.
(Oh heart, I do not dare go empty-hearted)
    I'll think of Love in books, Love without end;
Women with child, content; and old men sleeping;
    And wet strong ploughlands, scarred for certain grain;
And babes that weep, and so forget their weeping;
    And the young heavens, forgetful after rain;
And evening hush, broken by homing wings;
    And Song's nobility, and Wisdom holy,
That live, we dead. I would think of a thousand things,
    Lovely and durable, and taste them slowly,
One after one, like tasting a sweet food.
I have need to busy my heart with quietude.

RUPERT BROOKE

[41]

The Funeral of Youth: Threnody

THE day that *Youth* had died,
There came to his grave-side,
In decent mourning, from the country's ends,
Those scatter'd friends
Who had lived the boon companions of his prime,
And laughed with him and sung with him and wasted,
In feast and wine and many-crown'd carouse,
The days and nights and dawnings of the time
When *Youth* kept open house,
Nor left untasted
Aught of his high emprise and ventures dear,
No quest of his unshar'd —
All these, with loitering feet and sad head bar'd,
Followed their old friend's bier.
Folly went first,
With muffled bells and coxcomb still revers'd;
And after trod the bearers, hat in hand —
Laughter, most hoarse, and Captain *Pride* with tanned
And martial face all grim, and fussy *Joy*,
Who had to catch a train, and *Lust*, poor snivelling boy;
These bore the dear departed.
Behind them, broken-hearted,
Came *Grief*, so noisy a widow, that all said,
'Had he but wed
Her elder sister *Sorrow*, in her stead!'
And by her, trying to soothe her all the time,
The fatherless children, *Colour, Tune*, and *Rhyme*,
(The sweet lad *Rhyme*), ran all-uncomprehending.
Then, at the way's sad ending,
Round the raw grave they stay'd. Old *Wisdom* read
In mumbling tone the Service for the Dead.
There stood *Romance*,
The furrowing tears had mark'd her rougèd cheek;
Poor old *Conceit*, his wonder unassuag'd;
Dead *Innocency*'s daughter, *Ignorance*;
And shabby, ill-dress'd *Generosity*;
And *Argument*, too full of woe to speak;

Passion, grown portly, something middle-ag'd;
And *Friendship* – not a minute older, she;
Impatience, ever taking out his watch;
Faith, who was deaf, and had to lean, to catch
Old *Wisdom*'s endless drone.
Beauty was there,
Pale in her black; dry-eyed; she stood alone.
Poor maz'd *Imagination*; *Fancy* wild;
Ardour, the sunlight on his greying hair;
Contentment, who had known *Youth* as a child
And never seen him since. And *Spring* came too,
Dancing over the tombs, and brought him flowers –
She did not stay for long.
And *Truth*, and *Grace*, and all the merry crew,
The laughing *Winds* and *Rivers*, and lithe *Hours*;
And *Hope*, the dewy-eyed; and sorrowing *Song*; –
Yes, with much woe and mourning general,
At dead *Youth*'s funeral,
Even these were met once more together, all,
Who erst the fair and living *Youth* did know;
All, except only *Love*. *Love* had died long ago.

RUPERT BROOKE

Waterloo

There was a sound of revelry by night,
And Belgium's capital had gather'd then
Her Beauty and her Chivalry, and bright
The lamps shone o'er fair women and brave men;
A thousand hearts beat happily; and when
Music arose with its voluptuous swell,
Soft eyes look'd love to eyes which spake again,
And all went merry as a marriage bell;
But hush! hark! a deep sound strikes like a rising knell!

Did ye not hear it? – No; 'twas but the wind,
Or the car rattling o'er the stony street;
On with the dance! let joy be unconfined;
No sleep till morn, when Youth and Pleasure meet
To chase the glowing Hours with flying feet –
But hark! – that heavy sound breaks in once more,
As if the clouds its echo would repeat;
And nearer, clearer, deadlier than before!
Arm! Arm! it is – it is – the cannon's opening roar!

Within a window'd niche of that high hall
Sate Brunswick's fated chieftain; he did hear
That sound the first amidst the festival,
And caught its tone with Death's prophetic ear;
And when they smiled because he deem'd it near,
His heart more truly knew that peal too well
Which stretch'd his father on a bloody bier,
And roused the vengeance blood alone could quell;
He rush'd into the field, and, foremost fighting, fell.

Ah! then and there was hurrying to and fro,
And gathering tears, and tremblings of distress,
And cheeks all pale, which but an hour ago
Blush'd at the praise of their own loveliness;
And there were sudden partings, such as press
The life from out young hearts, and choking sighs
Which ne'er might be repeated; who could guess
If ever more should meet those mutual eyes,
Since upon night so sweet such awful morn could rise!

And there was mounting in hot haste: the steed,
The mustering squadron, and the clattering car,
Went pouring forward with impetuous speed,
And swiftly forming in the ranks of war;
And the deep thunder peal on peal afar;
And near, the beat of the alarming drum
Roused up the soldier ere the morning star;
While throng'd the citizens with terror dumb,
Or whispering, with white lips – 'The foe! they come! they come!'

And wild and high the 'Cameron's gathering' rose!
The war-note of Lochiel, which Albyn's hills
Have heard, and heard, too, have her Saxon foes: –
How in the noon of night that pibroch thrills,
Savage and shrill! But with the breath which fills
Their mountain-pipe, so fill the mountaineers
With the fierce native daring which instils
The stirring memory of a thousand years,
And Evan's, Donald's fame rings in each clansman's ears!

And Ardennes waves above them her green leaves,
Dewy with nature's tear-drops as they pass,
Grieving, if aught inanimate e'er grieves,
Over the unreturning brave, – alas!
Ere evening to be trodden like the grass
Which now beneath them, but above shall grow
In its next verdure, when this fiery mass
Of living vapour, rolling on the foe
And burning with high hope, shall moulder cold and low.

Last noon beheld them full of lusty life,
Last eve in Beauty's circle proudly gay,
The midnight brought the signal-sound of strife,
The morn the marshalling in arms, – the day
Battle's magnificently stern array!
The thunder-clouds close o'er it, which when rent
The earth is cover'd thick with other clay,
Which her own clay shall cover, heap'd and pent!
Rider and horse, – friend, foe, – in one red burial blent!

from *Childe Harold's Pilgrimage*. Canto III
LORD BYRON

[45]

Jabberwocky

'TWAS brillig, and the slithy toves
　　Did gyre and gimble in the wabe:
All mimsy were the borogoves,
　　And the mome raths outgrabe.

'Beware the Jabberwock, my son!
　　The jaws that bite, the claws that catch!
Beware the Jubjub bird, and shun
　　The frumious Bandersnatch!'

He took his vorpal sword in hand:
　　Long time the manxome foe he sought –
So rested he by the Tumtum tree,
　　And stood awhile in thought.

And, as in uffish thought he stood,
　　The Jabberwock, with eyes of flame,
Came whiffling through the tulgy wood,
　　And burbled as it came!

One, two! One, two! And through and through
　　The vorpal blade went snicker-snack!
He left it dead, and with its head
　　He went galumphing back.

'And hast thou slain the Jabberwock?
　　Come to my arms, my beamish boy!
O frabjous day! Callooh! Callay!'
　　He chortled in his joy.

'Twas brillig, and the slithy toves
　　Did gyre and gimble in the wabe:
All mimsy were the borogoves,
　　And the mome raths outgrabe.

LEWIS CARROLL

Invictus

Out of the night that covers me,
  Black as the Pit from pole to pole,
I thank whatever gods may be
  For my unconquerable soul.

In the fell clutch of circumstance
  I have not winced nor cried aloud.
Under the bludgeonings of chance
  My head is bloody, but unbowed.

Beyond this place of wrath and tears
  Looms but the horror of the shade,
And yet the menace of the years
  Finds, and shall find me, unafraid.

It matters not how strait the gate,
  How charged with punishments the scroll,
I am the master of my fate:
  I am the captain of my soul.

W.E. Henley

Inversnaid

ॐ

THIS darksome burn, horseback brown,
His rollrock highroad roaring down,
In coop and in comb the fleece of his foam
Flutes and low to the lake falls home.

A windpuff-bonnet of fáwn-fróth
Turns and twindles over the broth
Of a pool so pitchblack, féll-frówning,
It rounds and rounds Despair to drowning.

Degged with dew, dappled with dew
Are the groins of the braes that the brook treads through,
Wiry heathpacks, flitches of fern,
And the beadbonny ash that sits over the burn.

What would the world be, once bereft
Of wet and of wildness? Let them be left,
O let them be left, wildness and wet;
Long live the weeds and the wilderness yet.

GERARD MANLEY HOPKINS

A St Helena Lullaby

'How far is St Helena from a little child at play?'
What makes you want to wander there with all the world
    between?
Oh, Mother, call your son again or else he'll run away.
(*No one thinks of winter when the grass is green!*)

'How far is St Helena from a fight in Paris street?'
I haven't time to answer now – the men are falling fast.
The guns begin to thunder, and the drums begin to beat.
(*If you take the first step, you will take the last!*)

'How far is St Helena from the field of Austerlitz?'
You couldn't hear me if I told – so loud the cannons roar.
But not so far for people who are living by their wits.
(*'Gay go up' means 'Gay go down' the wide world o'er!*)

'How far is St Helena from an Emperor of France?'
I cannot see – I cannot tell – the crowns they dazzle so.
The Kings sit down to dinner, and the Queens stand up
    to dance.
(*After open weather you may look for snow!*)

'How far is St Helena from the Capes of Trafalgar?'
A longish way – a longish way – with ten year more to
    run.
It's South across the water underneath a falling star.
(*What you cannot finish you must leave undone!*)

'How far is St Helena from the Beresina ice?'
An ill way – a chill way – the ice begins to crack.
But not so far for gentlemen who never took advice.
(*When you can't go forward you must e'en come back!*)

'How far is St Helena from the field of Waterloo?'
A near way – a clear way – the ship will take you soon.
A pleasant place for gentlemen with little left to do.
(*Morning never tries you till the afternoon!*)

'How far from St Helena to the Gate of Heaven's Grace?'
That no one knows – that no one knows – and no one ever will.
But fold your hands across your heart and cover up your face,
And after all your trapesings, child, lie still!

RUDYARD KIPLING

Vespers

ନ୍ଦ

Little Boy kneels at the foot of the bed,
Droops on the little hands little gold head.
Hush! Hush! Whisper who dares!
Christopher Robin is saying his prayers.

God bless Mummy. I know that's right.
Wasn't it fun in the bath to-night?
The cold's so cold, and the hot's so hot.
Oh! *God bless Daddy* – I quite forgot.

If I open my fingers a little bit more,
I can see Nanny's dressing-gown on the door.
It's a beautiful blue, but it hasn't a hood.
Oh! *God bless Nanny and make her good.*

Mine has a hood, and I lie in bed,
And pull the hood right over my head,
And I shut my eyes, and I curl up small,
And nobody knows that I'm there at all.

Oh! *Thank you, God, for a lovely day.*
And what was the other I had to say?
I said 'Bless Daddy,' so what can it be?
Oh! Now I remember it. *God bless Me.*

Little Boy kneels at the foot of the bed,
Droops on the little hands little gold head.
Hush! Hush! Whisper who dares!
Christopher Robin is saying his prayers.

A.A. MILNE

The Law The Lawyers Know About

THE law the lawyers know about
Is property and land;
But why the leaves are on the trees,
And why the wind disturbs the seas,
Why honey is the food of bees,
Why horses have such tender knees,
Why winters come and rivers freeze,
Why Faith is more than what one sees,
And Hope survives the worst disease,
And Charity is more than these,
They do not understand.

H.D.C. PEPLER

Sonnet 104

To me, fair friend, you never can be old,
For as you were when first your eye I eyed,
Such seems your beauty still. Three winters cold
Have from the forests shook three summers' pride,
Three beauteous springs to yellow autumn turn'd
In process of the seasons have I seen,
Three April perfumes in three hot Junes burn'd,
Since first I saw you fresh, which yet are green.
Ah, yet doth beauty, like a dial-hand,
Steal from his figure, and no pace perceived;
So your sweet hue, which methinks still doth stand,
Hath motion, and mine eye may be deceived:
 For fear of which, hear this, thou age unbred;
 Ere you were born was beauty's summer dead.

WILLIAM SHAKESPEARE

[53]

'Tomorrow, and Tomorrow, and Tomorrow'

TOMORROW, and tomorrow, and tomorrow,
Creeps in this petty pace from day to day,
To the last syllable of recorded time;
And all our yesterdays have lighted fools
The way to dusty death. Out, out, brief candle!
Life's but a walking shadow, a poor player,
That struts and frets his hour upon the stage,
And then is heard no more. It is a tale
Told by an idiot, full of sound and fury,
Signifying nothing.

from *Macbeth*, V.v.
WILLIAM SHAKESPEARE

To My Daughter

BRIGHT clasp of her whole hand around my finger
My daughter, as we walk together now.
All my life I'll feel a ring invisibly
Circle this bone with shining: when she is grown
Far from today as her eyes are far already.

STEPHEN SPENDER

'A slumber did my spirit seal'

A SLUMBER did my spirit seal,
  I had no human fears:
She seemed a thing that could not feel
  The touch of earthly years.

No motion has she now, no force;
  She neither hears nor sees;
Rolled round in earth's diurnal course,
  With rocks, and stones, and trees.

WILLIAM WORDSWORTH

He Wishes for the Cloths
of Heaven

HAD I the heavens' embroidered cloths,
Enwrought with golden and silver light,
The blue and the dim and the dark cloths
Of night and light and the half-light,
I would spread the cloths under your feet:
But I, being poor, have only my dreams;
I have spread my dreams under your feet;
Tread softly because you tread on my dreams.

WILLIAM BUTLER YEATS

[57]

To an Adopted Child

Not flesh of my flesh
Nor bone of my bone
But still totally my own.
Never forget
For a single minute
You didn't grow under my heart
But in it.

ANONYMOUS

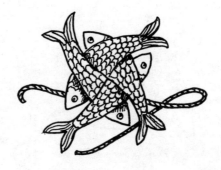

Preparations

Yet if His Majesty, our sovereign lord,
Should of his own accord
Friendly himself invite,
And say 'I'll be your guest to-morrow night,'
How should we stir ourselves, call and command
All hands to work! 'Let no man idle stand!
Set me fine Spanish tables in the hall;
See they be fitted all;
Let there be room to eat
And order taken that there want no meat.
See every sconce and candlestick made bright,
That without tapers they may give a light.
Look to the presence: are the carpets spread,
The dazie o'er the head,
The cushions in the chairs,
And all the candles lighted on the stairs?
Perfume the chambers, and in any case
Let each man give attendance in his place!'
Thus, if the king were coming, would we do,
And 'twere good reason too;
For 'tis a duteous thing
To show all honour to an earthly king,
And after all our travail and our cost,
So he be pleased, to think no labour lost.
But at the coming of the King of Heaven
All's set at six and seven;
We wallow in our sin,
Christ cannot find a chamber in the inn.
We entertain him always like a stranger,
And, as at first, still lodge him in the manger.

ANONYMOUS

Indoor Games Near Newbury

In among the silver birches winding ways of tarmac wander
   And the signs to Bussock Bottom, Tussock Wood and Windy
      Brake,
Gabled lodges, tile-hung churches, catch the lights of our Lagonda
   As we drive to Wendy's party, lemon curd and Christmas cake.
     Rich the makes of motor whirring,
     Past the pine-plantation purring
        Come up, Hupmobile, Delage!
Short the way your chauffeurs travel,
     Crunching over private gravel
        Each from out his warm garáge.

Oh but Wendy, when the carpet yielded to my indoor pumps
     There you stood, your gold hair streaming,
     Handsome in the hall-light gleaming
There you looked and there you led me off into the game of clumps
     Then the new Victrola playing
     And your funny uncle saying
'Choose your partners for a fox-trot! Dance until its *tea* o'clock!'
     'Come on, young 'uns, foot it featly!'
     Was it chance that paired us neatly,
     I, who loved you so completely,
You, who pressed me closely to you, hard against your party frock?
'Meet me when you've finished eating!' So we met and no one found us.
   Oh that dark and furry cupboard while the rest played hide and seek!
Holding hands our two hearts beating in the bedroom silence round us,
   Holding hands and hardly hearing sudden footstep, thud and shriek.
     Love that lay too deep for kissing –
     'Where *is* Wendy? Wendy's missing!'
       Love so pure it *had* to end,
     Love so strong that I was frighten'd
     When you gripped my fingers tight and
Hugging, whispered 'I'm your friend.'

Good-bye Wendy! Send the fairies, pinewood elf and larch tree
 gnome,
  Spingle-spangled stars are peeping
  At the lush Lagonda creeping
Down the winding ways of tarmac to the leaded lights of home.
  There, among the silver birches,
  All the bells of all the churches
Sounded in the bath-waste running out into the frosty air.
  Wendy speeded my undressing,
  Wendy is the sheet's caressing
  Wendy bending gives a blessing,
Holds me as I drift to dreamland, safe inside my slumber-wear.

JOHN BETJEMAN

from The Secret

For Mercy, Courage, Kindness, Mirth,
There is no measure upon earth.
Nay, they wither, root and stem,
If an end be set to them.

Overbrim and overflow
If your own heart you would know.
For the spirit, born to bless,
Lives but in its own excess.

Laurence Binyon

In the Dordogne

WE stood up before day
and shaved by metal mirrors
in the faint flame of a faulty candle.

And we hurried down the wide stone stairs
with a clirr of spur chains
on stone. And we thought
when the cocks crew
that the ghosts of a dead dawn
would rise and be off. But they stayed
under the window, crouched on the staircase,
the window now the colour of morning.

The colonel slept in the bed of Sully
slept on: but we descended
and saw in a niche in the white wall
a Virgin and child, serene
who were stone: we saw sycamores:
three aged mages
scattering gifts of gold.
But when the wind blew, there were autumn odours
and the shadowed trees
had the dapplings of young fawns.

And each day one died or another
died: each week we sent out thousands
that returned by hundreds
wounded or gassed. And those that died
We buried close to the old wall
within a stone's throw of Perigord
under the tower of the troubadours.

And because we had courage;
because there was courage and youth
ready to be wasted; because we endured
and were prepared for all endurance;
we thought something must come of it:
that the Virgin would raise her child and smile;
the trees gather up their gold and go;
that courage would avail something
and something we had never lost
be regained through wastage, by dying,
by burying the others under the English tower.

The colonel slept on in the bed of Sully
under the ravelling curtains: the leaves fell
and were blown away: the young men rotted
under the shadow of the tower
in a land of small clear silent streams
where the coming on of evening is
the letting down of blue and azure veils
over the clear and silent streams
delicately bordered by poplars.

JOHN PEALE BISHOP

from *Bishop Blougram's Apology*

No more wine? then we'll push back chairs and talk.
A final glass for me, though: cool, i' faith!
We ought to have our Abbey back, you see.
It's different, preaching in basilicas,
And doing duty in some masterpiece
Like this of brother Pugin's, bless his heart!
I doubt if they're half baked, those chalk rosettes,
Ciphers and stucco-twiddlings everywhere;
It's just like breathing in a lime-kiln: eh?
These hot long ceremonies of our church
Cost us a little – oh, they pay the price,
You take me – amply pay it! Now, we'll talk.

So, you despise me, Mr Gigadibs.
No deprecation, – nay, I beg you, sir!
Beside 'tis our engagement: don't you know,
I promised, if you'd watch a dinner out,
We'd see truth dawn together? – truth that peeps
Over the glasses' edge when dinner's done,
And body gets its sop and holds its noise
And leaves soul free a little. Now's the time:
Truth's break of day! You do despise me then.
And if I say, 'despise me,' – never fear!
I know you do not in a certain sense –
Not in my arm-chair, for example: here,
I well imagine you respect my place
(*Status, entourage,* worldly circumstance)
Quite to its value – very much indeed:
– Are up to the protesting eyes of you
In pride at being seated here for once –
You'll turn it to such capital account!
When somebody, through years and years to come,
Hints of the bishop, – names me – that's enough:
'Blougram? I knew him' – (into it you slide)
'Dined with him once, a Corpus Christi Day,
All alone, we two; he's a clever man:
And after dinner, – why, the wine you know, –

Oh, there was wine, and good! – what with the wine . . .
'Faith, we began upon all sorts of talk!
He's no bad fellow, Blougram; he had seen
Something of mine he relished, some review:
He's quite above their humbug in his heart,
Half-said as much, indeed – the thing's his trade.
I warrant, Blougram's sceptical at times:
How otherwise? I liked him, I confess!'
Che che, my dear sir, as we say at Rome,
Don't you protest now! It's fair give and take;
You have had your turn and spoken your home-truths:
The hand's mine now, and here you follow suit . . .

ROBERT BROWNING

A Grammarian's Funeral

Time: shortly after the revival of learning in Europe

LET us begin and carry up this corpse,
    Singing together.
Leave we the common crofts, the vulgar thorpes
    Each in its tether
Sleeping safe on the bosom of the plain,
    Cared-for till cock-crow:
Look out if yonder be not day again
    Rimming the rock-row!
That's the appropriate country; there, man's thought,
    Rarer, intenser,
Self-gathered for an outbreak, as it ought,
    Chafes in the censer.
Leave we the unlettered plain its herd and crop;
    Seek we sepulture
On a tall mountain, citied to the top,
    Crowded with culture!
All the peaks soar, but one the rest excels;
    Clouds overcome it;
No! yonder sparkle is the citadel's
    Circling its summit.
Thither our path lies; wind we up the heights:
    Wait ye the warning?
Our low life was the level's and the night's;
    He's for the morning.
Step to a tune, square chests, erect each head,
    'Ware the beholders!
This is our master, famous, calm and dead,
    Borne on our shoulders.

Sleep, crop and herd! sleep, darkling thorpe and croft,
    Safe from the weather!
He, whom we convoy to his grave aloft,
    Singing together,

He was a man born with thy face and throat,
　　Lyric Apollo!
Long he lived nameless: how should spring take note
　　Winter would follow?
Till lo, the little touch, and youth was gone!
　　Cramped and diminished,
Moaned he, 'New measures, other feet anon!
　　My dance is finished?'
No, that's the world's way: (keep the mountain-side,
　　Make for the city!)
He knew the signal, and stepped on with pride
　　Over men's pity;
Left play for work, and grappled with the world
　　Bent on escaping:
'What's in the scroll,' quoth he, 'thou keepest furled?
　　Show me their shaping,
Theirs who most studied man, the bard and sage, –
　　Give!' – So, he gowned him,
Straight got by heart that book to its last page:
　　Learned, we found him.
Yea, but we found him bald too, eyes like lead,
　　Accents uncertain:
'Time to taste life,' another would have said,
　　'Up with the curtain!'
This man said rather, 'Actual life comes next?
　　Patience a moment!
Grant I have mastered learning's crabbed text,
　　Still there's the comment.
Let me know all! Prate not of most or least,
　　Painful or easy!
Even to the crumbs I'd fain eat up the feast,
　　Ay, nor feel queasy.'
Oh, such a life as he resolved to live,
　　When he had learned it,
When he had gathered all books had to give!
　　Sooner, he spurned it.
Image the whole, then execute the parts –
　　Fancy the fabric
Quite, ere you build, ere steel strike fire from quartz,
　　Ere mortar dab brick!

(Here's the town-gate reached: there's the market-place
        Gaping before us.)
Yea, this in him was the peculiar grace
        (Hearten our chorus!)
That before living he'd learn how to live –
        No end to learning:
Earn the means first – God surely will contrive
        Use for our earning.
Others mistrust and say, 'But time escapes:
        Live now or never!'
He said, 'What's time? Leave Now for dogs and apes!
        Man has Forever.'
Back to his book then: deeper drooped his head:
        Calculus racked him:
Leaden before, his eyes grew dross of lead:
        Tussis attacked him.
'Now, master, take a little rest!' – not he!
        (Caution redoubled,
Step two abreast, the way winds narrowly!)
        Not a whit troubled
Back to his studies, fresher than at first,
        Fierce as a dragon
He (soul-hydroptic with a sacred thirst)
        Sucked at the flagon.
Oh, if we draw a circle premature,
        Heedless of far gain,
Greedy for quick returns of profit, sure
        Bad is our bargain!
Was it not great? did not he throw on God,
        (He loves the burthen) –
God's task to make the heavenly period
        Perfect the earthen?
Did not he magnify the mind, show clear
        Just what it all meant?
He would not discount life, as fools do here,
        Paid by instalment.
He ventured neck or nothing – heaven's success
        Found, or earth's failure:
'Wilt thou trust death or not?' He answered 'Yes:
        Hence with life's pale lure!'
That low man seeks a little thing to do,
        Sees it and does it:

This high man, with a great thing to pursue,
     Dies ere he knows it.
That low man goes on adding one to one,
     His hundred's soon hit:
This high man, aiming at a million,
     Misses an unit.
That, has the world here – should he need the next,
     Let the world mind him!
This, throws himself on God, and unperplexed
     Seeking shall find him.
So, with the throttling hands of death at strife,
     Ground he at grammar;
Still, thro' the rattle, parts of speech were rife:
     While he could stammer
He settled *Hoti*'s business – let it be! –
     Properly based *Oun* –
Gave us the doctrine of the enclitic *De*,
     Dead from the waist down.
Well, here's the platform, here's the proper place:
     Hail to your purlieus,
All ye highfliers of the feathered race,
     Swallows and curlews!
Here's the top-peak; the multitude below
     Live, for they can, there:
This man decided not to Live but Know –
     Bury this man there?
Here – here's his place, where meteors shoot, clouds form,
     Lightnings are loosened,
Stars come and go! Let joy break with the storm,
     Peace let the dew send!
Lofty designs must close in like effects:
     Loftily lying,
Leave him – still loftier than the world suspects,
     Living and dying.

ROBERT BROWNING

Porphyria's Lover

THE rain set early in to-night,
   The sullen wind was soon awake,
It tore the elm-tops down for spite,
   And did its worst to vex the lake:
   I listened with heart fit to break.
When glided in Porphyria; straight
   She shut the cold out and the storm,
And kneeled and made the cheerless grate
   Blaze up, and all the cottage warm;
   Which done, she rose, and from her form
Withdrew the dripping cloak and shawl,
   And laid her soiled gloves by, untied
Her hat and let the damp hair fall,
   And, last, she sat down by my side
   And called me. When no voice replied,
She put my arm about her waist,
   And made her smooth white shoulder bare,
And all her yellow hair displaced,
   And, stooping, made my cheek lie there,
   And spread, o'er all, her yellow hair,
Murmuring how she loved me – she
   Too weak, for all her heart's endeavour,
To set its struggling passion free
   From pride, and vainer ties dissever,
   And give herself to me for ever.
But passion sometimes would prevail,
   Nor could to-night's gay feast restrain
A sudden thought of one so pale
   For love of her, and all in vain:
   So, she was come through wind and rain.
Be sure I looked up at her eyes
   Happy and proud; at last I knew
Porphyria worshipped me; surprise
   Made my heart swell, and still it grew
   While I debated what to do.
That moment she was mine, mine, fair,
   Perfectly pure and good: I found

A thing to do, and all her hair
  In one long yellow string I wound
  Three times her little throat around,
And strangled her. No pain felt she;
  I am quite sure she felt no pain.
As a shut bud that holds a bee,
  I warily oped her lids: again
  Laughed the blue eyes without a stain.
And I untightened next the tress
  About her neck; her cheek once more
Blushed bright beneath my burning kiss:
  I propped her head up as before,
  Only, this time my shoulder bore
Her head, which droops upon it still:
  The smiling rosy little head,
So glad it has its utmost will,
  That all it scorned at once is fled,
  And I, its love, am gained instead!
Porphyria's love: she guessed not how
  Her darling one wish would be heard.
And thus we sit together now,
  And all night long we have not stirred,
  And yet God has not said a word!

ROBERT BROWNING

'Because I could not stop for Death'

BECAUSE I could not stop for Death –
He kindly stopped for me –
The Carriage held but just Ourselves –
And Immortality.

We slowly drove – He knew no haste
And I had put away
My labor and my leisure too,
For His Civility –

We passed the School, where Children strove
At Recess – in the Ring –
We passed the Fields of Gazing Grain –
We passed the Setting Sun –

Or rather – He passed Us –
The Dews drew quivering and chill –
For only Gossamer, my Gown –
My Tippet – only Tulle –

We paused before a House that seemed
A Swelling of the Ground –
The Roof was scarcely visible –
The Cornice – in the Ground –

Since then – 'tis Centuries – and yet
Feels shorter than the Day
I first surmised the Horses' Heads
Were toward Eternity –

EMILY DICKINSON

'At the round earths imagin'd corners'

AT the round earths imagin'd corners, blow
Your trumpets, Angells, and arise, arise
From death, you numberlesse infinities
Of soules, and to your scattred bodies goe,
All whom the flood did, and fire shall o'erthrow,
All whom warre, dearth, age, agues, tyrannies,
Despaire, law, chance, hath slaine, and you whose eyes,
Shall behold God, and never tast deaths woe.
But let them sleepe, Lord, and mee mourne a space,
For, if above all these, my sinnes abound,
'Tis late to aske abundance of thy grace,
When wee are there; here on this lowly ground,
Teach mee how to repent; for that's as good
As if thou'hadst seal'd my pardon, with thy blood.

JOHN DONNE

The Lion and Albert

ᘍ

THERE'S a famous seaside place called Blackpool,
    That's noted for fresh air and fun,
And Mr and Mrs Ramsbottom
    Went there with young Albert, their son.

A grand little lad was young Albert,
    All dressed in his best; quite a swell
With a stick with an 'orse's 'ead 'andle,
    The finest that Woolworth's could sell.

They didn't think much to the Ocean:
    The waves, they was fiddlin' and small,
There was no wrecks and nobody drownded,
    Fact, nothing to laugh at at all.

So, seeking for further amusement,
    They paid and went into the Zoo,
Where they'd Lions and Tigers and Camels,
    And old ale and sandwiches too.

There was one great big Lion called Wallace;
    His nose were all covered with scars –
He lay in a somnolent posture
    With the side of his face on the bars.

Now Albert had heard about Lions,
    How they was ferocious and wild –
To see Wallace lying so peaceful,
    Well, it didn't seem right to the child.

So straightway the brave little feller,
    Not showing a morsel of fear,
Took his stick with its 'orse's 'ead 'andle
    And pushed it in Wallace's ear.

You could see that the Lion didn't like it,
    For giving a kind of a roll,
He pulled Albert inside the cage with 'im,
    And swallowed the little lad 'ole.

Then Pa, who had seen the occurrence,
    And didn't know what to do next,
Said 'Mother! Yon Lion's 'et Albert,'
    And Mother said 'Well, I am vexed!'

Then Mr and Mrs Ramsbottom –
    Quite rightly, when all's said and done –
Complained to the Animal Keeper
    That the Lion had eaten their son.

The keeper was quite nice about it:
    He said 'What a nasty mishap.
Are you sure that it's your boy he's eaten?'
    Pa said 'Am I sure? There's his cap!'

The manager had to be sent for.
    He came and he said 'What's to do?'
Pa said 'Yon Lion's 'et Albert,
    And 'im in his Sunday clothes, too.'

Then Mother said, 'Right's right, young feller;
    I think it's a shame and a sin
For a lion to go and eat Albert,
    And after we've paid to come in.'

The manager wanted no trouble,
    He took out his purse right away,
Saying 'How much to settle the matter?'
    And Pa said 'What do you usually pay?'

But Mother had turned a bit awkward
    When she thought where her Albert had gone.
She said 'No! someone's got to be summonsed' –
    So that was decided upon.

Then off they went to the P'lice Station,
    In front of the Magistrate chap;
They told 'im what happened to Albert,
    And proved it by showing his cap.

The Magistrate gave his opinion
  That no one was really to blame
And he said that he hoped the Ramsbottoms
  Would have further sons to their name.

At that Mother got proper blazing,
  'And thank you, sir, kindly,' said she.
'What, waste all our lives raising children
  To feed ruddy Lions? Not me!'

MARRIOTT EDGAR

Skimbleshanks: the Railway Cat

THERE's a whisper down the line at 11.39
When the Night Mail's ready to depart,
Saying 'Skimble where is Skimble has he gone to hunt the thimble?
We must find him or the train can't start.'
All the guards and all the porters and the stationmaster's daughters
They are searching high and low,
Saying 'Skimble where is Skimble for unless he's very nimble
Then the Night Mail just can't go.'
At 11.42 then the signal's overdue
And the passengers are frantic to a man –
Then Skimble will appear and he'll saunter to the rear:
He's been busy in the luggage van!
    He gives one flash of his glass-green eyes
        And the signal goes 'All Clear!'
    And we're off at last for the northern part
        Of the Northern Hemisphere!

You may say that by and large it is Skimble who's in charge
Of the Sleeping Car Express.
From the driver and the guards to the bagmen playing cards
He will supervise them all, more or less.
Down the corridor he paces and examines all the faces
Of the travellers in the First and in the Third;
He establishes control by a regular patrol
And he'd know at once if anything occurred.
He will watch you without winking and he sees what you are thinking
And it's certain that he doesn't approve
Of hilarity and riot, so the folk are very quiet
When Skimble is about and on the move.
    You can play no pranks with Skimbleshanks!
        He's a Cat that cannot be ignored;
    So nothing goes wrong on the Northern Mail
        When Skimbleshanks is aboard.

Oh it's very pleasant when you have found your little den
With your name written up on the door.
And the berth is very neat with a newly folded sheet
And there's not a speck of dust on the floor.

[78]

There is every sort of light – you can make it dark or bright:
There's a button that you turn to make a breeze.
There's a funny little basin you're supposed to wash your face in
And a crank to shut the window if you sneeze.
Then the guard looks in politely and will ask you very brightly
'Do you like your morning tea weak or strong?'
But Skimble's just behind him and was ready to remind him,
For Skimble won't let anything go wrong.
    And when you creep into your cosy berth
      And pull up the counterpane,
   You ought to reflect that it's very nice
   To know that you won't be bothered by mice –
   You can leave all that to the Railway Cat,
    The Cat of the Railway Train!

In the watches of the night he is always fresh and bright;
Every now and then he has a cup of tea
With perhaps a drop of Scotch while he's keeping on the watch,
Only stopping here and there to catch a flea.
You were fast asleep at Crewe and so you never knew
That he was walking up and down the station;
You were sleeping all the while he was busy at Carlisle,
Where he greets the stationmaster with elation.
But you saw him at Dumfries, where he summons the police
If there's anything they ought to know about:
When you get to Gallowgate there you do not have to wait –
For Skimbleshanks will help you to get out!
    He gives you a wave of his long brown tail
      Which says: 'I'll see you again!
    You'll meet without fail on the Midnight Mail
      The Cat of the Railway Train.'

T.S. ELIOT

[79]

Fire and Ice

ﾛﾊ

SOME say the world will end in fire,
Some say in ice.
From what I've tasted of desire
I hold with those who favor fire.
But if it had to perish twice,
I think I know enough of hate
To say that for destruction ice
Is also great
And would suffice.

ROBERT FROST

An Elegy Written in a Country Churchyard

THE *Curfeu* tolls the Knell of parting Day,
The lowing Herd winds slowly o'er the Lea,
The Plow-man homeward plods his weary Way,
And leaves the World to Darkness, and to me.

Now fades the glimmering Landscape on the Sight,
And all the Air a solemn Stillness holds;
Save where the Beetle wheels his droning Flight,
And drowsy Tinklings lull the distant Folds.

Save that from yonder Ivy-mantled Tow'r
The mopeing Owl does to the Moon complain
Of such as, wand'ring near her secret Bow'r,
Molest her ancient solitary Reign.

Beneath those rugged Elms, that Yew-Tree's Shade,
Where heaves the Turf in many a mould'ring Heap,
Each in his narrow Cell for ever laid,
The rude Forefathers of the Hamlet sleep.

The breezy Call of Incense-breathing Morn,
The Swallow twitt'ring from the Straw-built Shed,
The Cock's shrill Clarion, or the ecchoing Horn,
No more shall rouse them from their lowly Bed.

For them no more the blazing Hearth shall burn,
Or busy Housewife ply her Evening Care:
No Children run to lisp their Sire's Return,
Or climb his Knees the envied Kiss to share.

Oft did the Harvest to their Sickle yield,
Their Furrow oft the stubborn Glebe has broke;
How jocund did they drive their Team afield!
How bow'd the Woods beneath their sturdy Stroke!

Let not Ambition mock their useful Toil,
Their homely Joys and Destiny obscure;
Nor Grandeur hear with a disdainful Smile,
    The short and simple Annals of the Poor.
      The Boast of Heraldry, the Pomp of Pow'r,
    And all that Beauty, all that Wealth e'er gave,
    Awaits alike th'inevitable Hour.

The Paths of Glory lead but to the Grave.
   Nor you, ye Proud, impute to these the Fault,
If Mem'ry o'er their Tomb no Trophies raise,
Where thro' the long-drawn Isle and fretted Vault
The pealing Anthem swells the Note of Praise.

   Can storied Urn or animated Bust
Back to its Mansion call the fleeting Breath?
Can Honour's Voice provoke the silent Dust,
Or Flatt'ry sooth the dull cold Ear of Death?

   Perhaps in this neglected Spot is laid
Some Heart once pregnant with celestial Fire,
Hands that the Rod of Empire might have sway'd,
Or wak'd to Extacy the living Lyre.

   But Knowledge to their Eyes her ample Page
Rich with the Spoils of Time did ne'er unroll;
Chill Penury repress'd their noble Rage,
And froze the genial Current of the Soul.

   Full many a gem of purest Ray serene,
The dark unfathom'd Caves of Ocean bear:
Full many a Flower is born to blush unseen,
And waste its Sweetness on the desart Air.

   Some Village-*Hampden* that with dauntless Breast
The little Tyrant of his Fields withstood;
Some mute inglorious *Milton* here may rest,
Some *Cromwell* guiltless of his Country's Blood.

   Th'Applause of list'ning Senates to command,
The Threats of Pain and Ruin to despise,
To scatter Plenty o'er a smiling Land.
And read their Hist'ry in a Nation's Eyes,

   Their Lot forbad: nor circumscrib'd alone,
Their growing Virtues, but their Crimes confin'd;
Forbad to wade through Slaughter to a Throne,
And shut the Gates of Mercy on Mankind,

   The struggling Pangs of conscious Truth to hide,
To quench the Blushes of ingenuous Shame,
Or heap the Shrine of Luxury and Pride
With Incense, kindled at the Muse's Flame.

   Far from the madding Crowd's ignoble Strife
Their sober Wishes never learn'd to stray;
Along the cool sequester'd Vale of Life
They kept the noiseless Tenor of their Way.

Yet ev'n these Bones from Insult to protect
Some frail Memorial still erected nigh,
With uncouth Rhimes and shapeless Sculpture deck'd,
Implores the passing Tribute of a Sigh.

Their Name, their Years, spelt by th'unletter'd Muse,
The Place of Fame and Elegy supply:
And many a holy Text around she strews,
That teach the rustic Moralist to dye.

For who to dumb Forgetfulness a Prey,
This pleasing anxious Being e'er resign'd,
Left the warm Precincts of the chearful Day,
Nor cast one longing ling'ring Look behind?

On some fond Breast the parting Soul relies,
Some pious Drops the closing Eye requires;
Ev'n from the Tomb the Voice of Nature cries,
Ev'n in our Ashes live their wonted Fires.

For thee, who mindful of th'unhonour'd Dead
Dost in these Lines their artless Tale relate;
If chance, by lonely Contemplation led,
Some kindred Spirit shall inquire thy Fate,

Haply some hoary-headed Swain may say,
'Oft have we seen him at the Peep of Dawn
'Brushing with hasty Steps the Dews away
'To meet the Sun upon the upland Lawn.

'There at the Foot of yonder nodding Beech
'That wreathes its old fantastic Roots so high,
'His listless Length at Noontide wou'd he stretch,
'And pore upon the Brook that babbles by.

'Hard by yon Wood, now smiling as in Scorn,
'Mutt'ring his wayward Fancies he wou'd rove,
'Now drooping, woeful wan, like one forlorn,
'Or craz'd with Care, or cross'd in hopeless Love.

'One Morn I miss'd him on the custom'd Hill,
'Along the Heath, and near his fav'rite Tree;
'Another came; nor yet beside the Rill,
'Nor up the Lawn, nor at the Wood was he.

'The next with Dirges due in sad Array
'Slow thro' the Church-way Path we saw him born.
'Approach and read (for thou can'st read) the Lay,
'Grav'd on the Stone beneath yon aged Thorn.

(There scatter'd oft, the earliest of the Year,
By Hands unseen, are Show'rs of Violets found:
The Red-breast loves to bill and warble there,
And little Footsteps lightly print the Ground.)

    Here rests his Head upon the Lap of Earth
A Youth to Fortune and Faith unknown:
Fair Science frown'd not on his humble Birth,
And Melancholy mark'd him for her own.
    Large was his Bounty, and his Soul sincere,
Heav'n did a Recompence as largely send:
He gave to Mis'ry all he had, A Tear:
He gain'd from Heav'n ('twas all he wish'd) a Friend.
    No farther seek his Merits to disclose,
Or draw his Frailties from their dread Abode,
(There they alike in trembling Hope repose)
The Bosom of his Father and his God.

THOMAS GRAY

Clearances

In memoriam M.K.H., 1911–1984

―――――――――

She taught me what her uncle once taught her:
How easily the biggest coal block split
If you got the grain and hammer angled right.

The sound of that relaxed alluring blow,
Its co-opted and obliterated echo,
Taught me to hit, taught me to loosen,

Taught me between the hammer and the block
To face the music. Teach me now to listen,
To strike it rich behind the linear black.

In the last minutes he said more to her
Almost than in all their life together.
'You'll be in New Row on Monday night
And I'll come up for you and you'll be glad
When I walk in the door . . . Isn't that right?'
His head was bent down to her propped-up head.
She could not hear but we were overjoyed.
He called her good and girl. Then she was dead,
The searching for a pulsebeat was abandoned
And we all knew one thing by being there.
The space we stood around had been emptied
Into us to keep, it penetrated
Clearances that suddenly stood open.
High cries were felled and a pure change happened.

Seamus Heaney

'Dear Bankers, PAY the
undermentioned hounds'

Dear Bankers, PAY the undermentioned hounds
The shameful sum of FIVE-AND-EIGHTY-POUNDS £85.0.0
By 'hound', of course, by custom, one refers
To SPECIAL (INCOME TAX) COMMISSIONERS
And these progenitors of woe and worry
You'll find at LYNWOOD ROAD, THAMES DITTON,
    SURREY.
This is the *second* lot of tax, you know,
On money that I earned two years ago
(The shark, they say, by no means Nature's Knight,
Will rest contented with a single bite:
The barracuda, who's a fish more fell,
Comes back and takes the other leg as well).
Two years ago. But things have changed since then.
I've reached the age of three-score years and ten.
My earnings dwindle: and the kindly State
Gives me a tiny pension – with my mate.
You'd think the State would generously roar
'At least, he shan't pay SURTAX any more'.
Instead, by this unChristian attack
They get two-thirds of my poor pension back.
Oh, very well. No doubt it's for the best;
At all events, pray do as I request:
And let the good old customs be enforced –
Don't cash this cheque, unless it is endorsed.

A.P. HERBERT

Written as a cheque, duly stamped and crossed. He received a reply from the Office of
the Special Commissioners of Income Tax, printed on page 87.

'Dear Sir, it is with pleasure that I thank'

Dear Sir, it is with pleasure that I thank
You for your letter, and the order to your bank
To pay the sum of five and eighty pounds
To those here whom you designate as hounds.
Their appetite is satisfied. In fact
You paid too much and I am forced to act,
Not to repay you, as perchance you dream,
Though such a course is easy, it would seem.
Your liability for later years
Is giving your accountants many tears:
And till such time as they and we can come
To amicable settlement on the sum
That represents your tax-bill to the State
I'll leave the overpayment to its fate.
I do not think this step will make you frown:
The sum involved is only half-a-crown.
                              Yours faithfully,

                              A.L. Grove

A reply from the Office of the Special Commissioners of Income Tax to A.P.
Herbert's cheque on page 86. A.P. Herbert replied:

> I thank you, Sir, but am afraid
> Of such a rival in my trade:
> One never should encourage those –
> In future I shall pay in prose.

La Belle Dame sans Merci

O WHAT can ail thee, knight-at-arms,
    Alone and palely loitering?
The sedge has withered from the lake,
    And no birds sing.

O what can ail thee, knight-at-arms,
    So haggard and so woe-begone?
The squirrel's granary is full,
    And the harvest's done.

I see a lily on thy brow,
    With anguish moist and fever-dew,
And on thy cheeks a fading rose
    Fast withereth too.

I met a lady in the meads,
    Full beautiful – a faery's child,
Her hair was long, her foot was light,
    And her eyes were wild.

I made a garland for her head,
    And bracelets too, and fragrant zone;
She looked at me as she did love,
    And made sweet moan.

I set her on my pacing steed,
    And nothing else saw all day long,
For sidelong would she bend, and sing
    A faery's song.

She found me roots of relish sweet,
    And honey wild, and manna-dew,
And sure in language strange she said –
'I love thee true'.

She took me to her elfin grot,
    And there she wept and sighed full sore,
And there I shut her wild wild eyes
    With kisses four.

And there she lullèd me asleep
   And there I dreamed – Ah! woe betide! –
The latest dream I ever dreamt
   On the cold hill side.

I saw pale kings and princes too,
   Pale warriors, death-pale were they all;
They cried – 'La Belle Dame sans Merci
   Hath thee in thrall!'

I saw their starved lips in the gloam,
   With horrid warning gapèd wide,
And I awoke and found me here,
   On the cold hill's side.

And this is why I sojourn here
   Alone and palely loitering,
Though the sedge is withered from the lake,
   And no birds sing.

JOHN KEATS

from *The Eve of St Agnes*

Sᴛ Agnes' Eve – Ah, bitter chill it was!
The owl, for all his feathers, was a-cold;
The hare limped trembling through the frozen grass,
And silent was the flock in woolly fold:
Numb were the Beadsman's fingers, while he told
His rosary, and while his frosted breath,
Like pious incense from a censer old,
Seemed taking flight for heaven, without a death,
Past the sweet Virgin's picture, while his prayer he saith.

His prayer he saith, this patient, holy man;
Then takes his lamp, and riseth from his knees,
And back returneth, meagre, barefoot, wan,
Along the chapel aisle by slow degrees:
The sculptured dead, on each side, seem to freeze,
Emprisoned in black, purgatorial rails;
Knights, ladies, praying in dumb orat'ries,
He passeth by; and his weak spirit fails
To think how they may ache in icy hoods and mails.

Northward he turneth through a little door,
And scarce three steps, ere Music's golden tongue
Flattered to tears this agèd man and poor;
But no – already had his deathbell rung:
The joys of all his life were said and sung:
His was harsh penance on St Agnes' Eve.
Another way he went, and soon among
Rough ashes sat he for his soul's reprieve,
And all night kept awake, for sinners' sake to grieve.

That ancient Beadsman heard the prelude soft;
And so it chanced, for many a door was wide,
From hurry to and fro. Soon, up aloft,

The silver, snarling trumpets 'gan to chide:
The level chambers, ready with their pride,
Were glowing to receive a thousand guests:
The carvèd angels, ever eager-eyed,
Stared, where upon their heads the cornice rests,
With hair blown back, and wings put cross-wise on their breasts.

At length burst in the argent revelry,
With plume, tiara, and all rich array,
Numerous as shadows haunting faerily
The brain, new-stuffed, in youth, with triumphs gay
Of old romance. These let us wish away,
And turn, sole-thoughted, to one Lady there,
Whose heart had brooded, all that wintry day,
On love, and winged St Agnes' saintly care,
As she had heard old dames full many times declare.

They told her how, upon St Agnes' Eve,
Young virgins might have visions of delight,
And soft adorings from their loves receive
Upon the honeyed middle of the night,
If ceremonies due they did aright;
As, supperless to bed they must retire,
And couch supine their beauties, lily white;
Nor look behind, nor sideways, but require
Of Heaven with upward eyes for all that they desire.

Full of this whim was thoughtful Madeline:
The music, yearning like a God in pain,
She scarcely heard: her maiden eyes divine,
Fixed on the floor, saw many a sweeping train
Pass by – she heeded not at all: in vain
Came many a tip-toe, amorous cavalier,
And back retired – not cooled by high disdain,
But she saw not: her heart was otherwhere.
She sighed for Agnes' dreams, the sweetest of the year . . .

JOHN KEATS

Danny Deever

ᘐ

'WHAT are the bugles blowin' for?' said Files-on-Parade.
'To turn you out, to turn you out,' the Colour-Sergeant said.
'What makes you look so white, so white?' said Files-on-Parade.
'I'm dreadin' what I've got to watch,' the Colour-Sergeant said.
   For they're hangin' Danny Deever, you can hear the Dead March
      play,
   The regiment's in 'ollow square – they're hangin' him to-day;
   They've taken of his buttons off an' cut his stripes away,
   An' they're hangin' Danny Deever in the mornin'.

'What makes the rear-rank breathe so 'ard?' said Files-on-Parade.
'It's bitter cold, it's bitter cold,' the Colour-Sergeant said.
'What makes that front-rank man fall down?' said Files-on-Parade.
'A touch o' sun, a touch o' sun,' the Colour-Sergeant said.
   They are hangin' Danny Deever, they are marchin' of 'im round,
   They 'ave 'alted Danny Deever by 'is coffin on the ground;
   An' 'e'll swing in 'arf a minute for a sneakin' shootin' hound –
   O they're hangin' Danny Deever in the mornin'!

''Is cot was right-'and cot to mine,' said Files-on-Parade.
''E's sleepin' out an' far to-night,' the Colour-Sergeant said.
'I've drunk 'is beer a score o' times,' said Files-on-Parade.
''E's drinkin' bitter beer alone,' the Colour-Sergeant said.
   They are hangin' Danny Deever, you must mark 'im to 'is place,
   For 'e shot a comrade sleepin' – you must look 'im in the face;
   Nine 'undred of 'is county an' the Regiment's disgrace,
   While they're hangin' Danny Deever in the mornin'.

'What's that so black agin the sun?' said Files-on-Parade.
'It's Danny fightin' 'ard for life,' the Colour-Sergeant said.
'What's that what whimpers over'ead?' said Files-on-Parade.
'It's Danny's soul that's passin' now,' the Colour-Sergeant said.
    For they're done with Danny Deever, you can 'ear the quickstep play,
    The regiment's in column, an' they're marchin' us away;
    Ho! the young recruits are shakin', an' they'll want their beer to-day,
    After hangin' Danny Deever in the mornin'!

RUDYARD KIPLING

The Way Through the Woods

THEY shut the road through the woods
Seventy years ago.
Weather and rain have undone it again,
And now you would never know
There was once a road through the woods
Before they planted the trees.
It is underneath the coppice and heath
And the thin anemones.
Only the keeper sees
That, where the ring-dove broods,
And the badgers roll at ease,
There was once a road through the woods.

Yet, if you enter the woods
Of a summer evening late,
When the night-air cools on the trout-ringed pools
Where the otter whistles his mate,
(They fear not men in the woods,
Because they see so few.)
You will hear the beat of a horse's feet,
And the swish of a skirt in the dew,
Steadily cantering through
The misty solitudes,
As though they perfectly knew
The old lost road through the woods . . .
But there is no road through the woods.

RUDYARD KIPLING

Lays of Ancient Rome

I

LARS Porsena of Clusium
  By the Nine Gods he swore
That the great house of Tarquin
  Should suffer wrong no more.
By the Nine Gods he swore it,
  And named a trysting day,
And bade his messengers ride forth,
East and west and south and north,
  To summon his array.

II

East and west and south and north
  The messengers ride fast,
And tower and town and cottage
  Have heard the trumpet's blast.
Shame on the false Etruscan
  Who lingers in his home,
When Porsena of Clusium
  Is on the march for Rome.

III

The horsemen and the footmen
  Are pouring in amain
From many a stately market-place;
  From many a fruitful plain;
From many a lonely hamlet,
  Which, hid by beech and pine,
Like an eagle's nest, hangs on the crest
  Of purple Apennine; . . .

XI

And now hath every city
  Sent up her tale of men;

The foot are fourscore thousand,
　The horse are thousands ten:
Before the gates of Sutrium
　Is met the great array.
A proud man was Lars Porsena
　Upon the trysting day.

XII

For all the Etruscan armies
　Were ranged beneath his eye,
And many a banished Roman,
　And many a stout ally;
And with a mighty following
　To join the muster came
The Tusculan Mamilius,
　Prince of the Latian name.

XIII

But by the yellow Tiber
　Was tumult and affright:
From all the spacious champaign
　To Rome men took their flight.
A mile around the city,
　The throng stopped up the ways;
A fearful sight it was to see
　Through two long nights and days . . .

XIX

They held a council standing
　Before the River-Gate;
Short time was there, ye well may guess,
　For musing or debate.
Out spake the Consul roundly:
　'The bridge must straight go down;
For, since Janiculum is lost,
　Nought else can save the town.'

XX

Just then a scout came flying,
　All wild with haste and fear;
'To arms! to arms! Sir Consul:
　Lars Porsena is here.'

On the low hills to westward
    The Consul fixed his eye,
And saw the swarthy storm of dust
    Rise fast along the sky.

XXI

And nearer fast and nearer
    Doth the red whirlwind come;
And louder still and still more loud,
From underneath that rolling cloud,
Is heard the trumpet's war-note proud,
    The trampling, and the hum.
And plainly and more plainly
    Now through the gloom appears,
Far to left and far to right,
In broken gleams of dark-blue light,
The long array of helmets bright,
    The long array of spears.

XXII

And plainly and more plainly,
    Above that glimmering line,
Now might ye see the banners
    Of twelve fair cities shine;
But the banner of proud Clusium
    Was highest of them all,
The terror of the Umbrian,
    The terror of the Gaul . . .

XXVI

But the Consul's brow was sad,
    And the Consul's speech was low,
And darkly looked he at the wall,
    And darkly at the foe.
'Their van will be upon us
    Before the bridge goes down;
And if they once may win the bridge,
    What hope to save the town?'

XXVII

Then out spake brave Horatius,
    The Captain of the Gate:

[97]

'To every man upon this earth
   Death cometh soon or late.
And how can man die better
   Than facing fearful odds,
For the ashes of his fathers,
   And the temples of his Gods,

XXVIII

'And for the tender mother
   Who dandled him to rest,
And for the wife who nurses
   His baby at her breast,
And for the holy maidens
   Who feed the eternal flame,
To save them from false Sextus
   That wrought the deed of shame?

XXIX

'Hew down the bridge, Sir Consul,
   With all the speed ye may;
I, with two more to help me,
   Will hold the foe in play.
In yon strait path a thousand
   May well be stopped by three.
Now who will stand on either hand,
   And keep the bridge with me?'

XXX

Then out spake Spurius Lartius;
   A Ramnian proud was he:
'Lo, I will stand at thy right hand,
   And keep the bridge with thee.'
And out spake strong Herminius;
   Of Titian blood was he:
'I will abide on thy left side,
   And keep the bridge with thee.'

XXXI

'Horatius,' quoth the Consul,
   'As thou sayest, so let it be.'
And straight against that great array
   Forth went the dauntless Three.

For Romans in Rome's quarrel
  Spared neither land nor gold,
Nor son nor wife, nor limb nor life,
  In the brave days of old.

XXXII

Then none was for a party;
  Then all were for the state;
Then the great man helped the poor,
  And the poor man loved the great;
Then lands were fairly portioned;
  Then spoils were fairly sold;
The Romans were like brothers
  In the brave days of old.

XXXIII

Now Roman is to Roman
  More hateful than a foe,
And the Tribunes beard the high,
  And the Fathers grind the low.
As we wax hot in faction,
  In battle we wax cold;
Wherefore men fight not as they fought
  In the brave days of old.

XXXIV

Now while the Three were tightening
  Their harness on their backs,
The Consul was the foremost man
  To take in hand an axe:
And Fathers mixed with Commons
  Seized hatchet, bar, and crow,
And smote upon the planks above,
  And loosed the props below.

XXXV

Meanwhile the Tuscan army,
  Right glorious to behold,
Came flashing back the noonday light,
Rank behind rank, like surges bright
  Of a broad sea of gold . . .

Four hundred trumpets sounded
    A peal of warlike glee,
As that great host, with measured tread,
And spears advanced, and ensigns spread,
Rolled slowly towards the bridge's head,
    Where stood the dauntless Three.

L

Was none who would be foremost
    To lead such dire attack:
But those behind cried 'Forward!'
    And those before cried 'Back!'
And backward now and forward
    Wavers the deep array;
And on the tossing sea of steel,
    To and fro the standards reel;
And the victorious trumpet-peal
    Dies fitfully away.

LI

Yet one man for one moment
    Stood out before the crowd;
Well known was he to all the Three,
    And they gave him greeting loud,
'Now welcome, welcome, Sextus!
    Now welcome to thy home!
Why dost thou stay, and turn away?
    Here lies the road to Rome.'

LII

Thrice looked he at the city;
    Thrice looked he at the dead;
And thrice came on in fury,
    And thrice turned back in dread:
And, white with fear and hatred,
    Scowled at the narrow way
Where, wallowing in a pool of blood,
    The bravest Tuscans lay.

LIII

But meanwhile axe and lever
    Have manfully been plied;

And now the bridge hangs tottering
    Above the boiling tide.
'Come back, come back, Horatius!'
    Loud cried the Fathers all.
'Back, Lartius! back, Herminius!
    Back, ere the ruin fall!'

LIV

Back darted Spurius Lartius;
    Herminius darted back:
And as they passed, beneath their feet
    They felt the timbers crack.
But when they turned their faces,
    And on the farther shore
Saw brave Horatius stand alone,
    They would have crossed once more.

LV

But with a crash like thunder
    Fell every loosened beam,
And, like a dam, the mighty wreck
    Lay right athwart the stream:
And a long shout of triumph
    Rose from the walls of Rome,
As to the highest turret-tops
    Was splashed the yellow foam.

LVI

And, like a horse unbroken
    When first he feels the rein,
The furious river struggled hard,
    And tossed his tawny mane,
And burst the curb, and bounded,
    Rejoicing to be free,
And whirling down, in fierce career,
Battlement, and plank, and pier,
    Rushed headlong to the sea.

LVII

Alone stood brave Horatius,
    But constant still in mind;
Thrice thirty thousand foes before,

And the broad flood behind.
'Down with him!' cried false Sextus,
    With a smile on his pale face.
'Now yield thee,' cried Lars Porsena,
    'Now yield thee to our grace.'

LVIII

Round turned he, as not deigning
    Those craven ranks to see;
Nought spake he to Lars Porsena,
    To Sextus nought spake he;
But he saw on Palatinus
    The white porch of his home;
And he spake to the noble river
    That rolls by the towers of Rome.

LIX

'Oh, Tiber! father Tiber!
    To whom the Romans pray,
A Roman's life, a Roman's arms,
    Take thou in charge this day!'
So he spake, and speaking sheathed
    The good sword by his side,
And with his harness on his back,
    Plunged headlong in the tide.

LX

No sound of joy or sorrow
    Was heard from either bank;
But friends and foes in dumb surprise,
With parted lips and straining eyes,
    Stood gazing where he sank;
And when above the surges
    They saw his crest appear,
All Rome sent forth a rapturous cry,
And even the ranks of Tuscany
    Could scarce forbear to cheer.

LXI

But fiercely ran the current,
    Swollen high by months of rain:
And fast his blood was flowing;

And he was sore in pain,
And heavy with his armour,
   And spent with changing blows;
And oft they thought him sinking,
   But still again he rose.

LXII

Never, I ween, did swimmer,
   In such an evil case,
Struggle through such a raging flood
   Safe to the landing place:
But his limbs were borne up bravely
   By the brave heart within,
And our good father Tiber
   Bore bravely up his chin.

LXIII

'Curse on him!' quoth false Sextus;
   'Will not the villain drown?
But for this stay, ere close of day
   We should have sacked the town!'
'Heaven help him!' quoth Lars Porsena,
   'And bring him safe to shore;
For such a gallant feat of arms
   Was never seen before.'

LXIV

And now he feels the bottom;
   Now on dry earth he stands;
Now round him throng the Fathers
   To press his gory hands;
And now, with shouts and clapping,
   And noise of weeping loud,
He enters through the River-Gate,
   Borne by the joyous crowd.

LXV

They gave him of the corn-land,
   That was of public right,
As much as two strong oxen
   Could plough from morn till night;
And they made a molten image,

And set it up on high,
And there it stands unto this day
    To witness if I lie.

LXVI

It stands in the Comitium,
    Plain for all folk to see;
Horatius in his harness,
    Halting upon one knee:
And underneath is written,
    In letters all of gold,
How valiantly he kept the bridge
    In the brave days of old.

from *Horatius*
THOMAS BABINGTON MACAULAY

from *Prometheus Unbound: Act I*

SCENE *A Ravine of Icy Rocks in the Indian Caucasus.* PROMETHEUS *is discovered bound to the Precipice.* PANTHEA *and* IONE *are seated at his feet. Time, night. During the Scene, morning slowly breaks.*

PROMETHEUS Monarch of Gods and Daemons, and all Spirits
But One, who throng those bright and rolling worlds
Which Thou and I alone of living things
Behold with sleepless eyes! regard this Earth
Made multitudinous with thy slaves, whom thou
Requitest for knee-worship, prayer, and praise,
And toil, and hecatombs of broken hearts,
With fear and self-contempt and barren hope.
Whilst me, who am thy foe, eyeless in hate,
Hast thou made reign and triumph, to thy scorn,
O'er mine own misery and thy vain revenge.
Three thousand years of sleep-unsheltered hours,
And moments aye divided by keen pangs
Till they seemed years, torture and solitude,
Scorn and despair, – these are mine empire: –
More glorious far than that which thou surveyest
From thine unenvied throne, O Mighty God!
Almighty, had I deigned to share the shame
Of thine ill tyranny, and hung not here
Nailed to this wall of eagle-baffling mountain,
Black, wintry, dead, unmeasured; without herb,
Insect, or beast, or shape or sound of life.
Ah me! alas, pain, pain ever, forever!

No change, no pause, no hope! Yet I endure.
I ask the Earth, have not the mountains felt?
I ask yon Heaven, the all-beholding Sun,
Has it not seen? The sea, in storm or calm,
Heaven's ever-changing Shadow, spread below,
Have its deaf waves not heard my agony?
Ah me! alas, pain, pain ever, forever!

The crawling glaciers pierce me with the spears
Of their moon-freezing crystals, the bright chains
Eat with their burning cold into my bones.

Heaven's wingèd hound, polluting from thy lips
His beak in poison not his own, tears up
My heart; and shapeless sights come wandering by,
The ghastly people of the realm of dream,
Mocking me: and the Earthquake-fiends are charged
To wrench the rivets from my quivering wounds
When the rocks split and close again behind:
While from their loud abysses howling throng
The genii of the storm, urging the rage
Of whirlwind, and afflict me with keen hail.
And yet to me welcome is day and night,
Whether one breaks the hoar frost of the morn,
Or starry, dim, and slow, the other climbs
The leaden-coloured east; for then they lead
The wingless, crawling hours, one among whom
– As some dark Priest hales the reluctant victim –
Shall drag thee, cruel King, to kiss the blood
From these pale feet, which then might trample thee
If they disdained not such a prostrate slave.
Disdain! Ah no! I pity thee. What ruin
Will hunt thee undefended through wide Heaven!
How will thy soul, cloven to its depth with terror,
Gape like a hell within! I speak in grief,
Not exultation, for I hate no more,
As then ere misery made me wise. The curse
Once breathed on thee I would recall. Ye Mountains,
Whose many-voicèd Echoes, through the mist
Of cataracts, flung the thunder of that spell!
Ye icy Springs, stagnant with wrinkling frost,
Which vibrated to hear me, and then crept
Shuddering through India! Thou serenest Air,
Through which the Sun walks burning without beams!
And ye swift Whirlwinds, who on poisèd wings
Hung mute and moveless o'er yon hushed abyss,
As thunder, louder than your own, made rock
The orbèd world! If then my words had power,
Though I am changed so that aught evil wish
Is dead within; although no memory be
Of what is hate, let them not lose it now!
What was that curse? for ye all heard me speak.

PERCY BYSSHE SHELLEY

Tithonus

THE woods decay, the woods decay and fall,
The vapours weep their burthen to the ground,
Man comes and tills the field and lies beneath,
And after many a summer dies the swan.
Me only cruel immortality
Consumes: I wither slowly in thine arms,
Here at the quiet limit of the world,
A white-hair'd shadow roaming like a dream
The ever silent spaces of the East,
Far-folded mists, and gleaming halls of morn.

    Alas! for this grey shadow, once a man –
So glorious in his beauty and thy choice,
Who madest him thy chosen, that he seem'd
To his great heart none other than a God!
I ask'd thee, 'Give me immortality.'
Then didst thou grant mine asking with a smile,
Like wealthy men who care not how they give.
But thy strong Hours indignant work'd their wills,
And beat me down and marr'd and wasted me,
And tho' they could not end me, left me maim'd
To dwell in presence of immortal youth,
Immortal age beside immortal youth,
And all I was, in ashes. Can thy love,
Thy beauty, make amends, tho' even now,
Close over us, the silver star, thy guide,
Shines in those tremulous eyes that fill with tears
To hear me? Let me go: take back thy gift:
Why should a man desire in any way
To vary from the kindly race of men,
Or pass beyond the goal of ordinance
Where all should pause, as is most meet for all?

    A soft air fans the cloud apart; there comes
A glimpse of that dark world where I was born.
Once more the old mysterious glimmer steals
From thy pure brows, and from thy shoulders pure,
And bosom beating with a heart renew'd.

Thy cheek begins to redden thro' the gloom,
Thy sweet eyes brighten slowly close to mine,
Ere yet they blind the stars, and the wild team
Which love thee, yearning for thy yoke, arise,
And shake the darkness from their loosen'd manes,
And beat the twilight into flakes of fire.

Lo! ever thus thou growest beautiful
In silence, then before thine answer given
Departest, and thy tears are on my cheek.

Why wilt thou ever scare me with thy tears,
And make me tremble lest a saying learnt
In days far-off, on that dark earth, be true?
'The Gods themselves cannot recall their gifts.'

Ay me! ay me! with what another heart
In days far-off, and with what other eyes
I used to watch – if I be he that watch'd –
The lucid outline forming round thee; saw
The dim curls kindle into sunny rings;
Changed with thy mystic change, and felt my blood
Glow with the glow that slowly crimson'd all
Thy presence and thy portals, while I lay,
Mouth, forehead, eyelids, growing dewy-warm
With kisses balmier than half-opening buds
Of April, and could hear the lips that kiss'd
Whispering I knew not what of wild and sweet,
Like that strange song I heard Apollo sing,
While Ilion like a mist rose into towers.

Yet hold me not for ever in thine East:
How can my nature longer mix with thine?
Coldly thy rosy shadows bathe me, cold
Are all thy lights, and cold my wrinkled feet
Upon thy glimmering thresholds, when the steam
Floats up from those dim fields about the homes
Of happy men that have the power to die,
And grassy barrows of the happier dead.
Release me, and restore me to the ground;
Thou seëst all things, thou wilt see my grave:
Thou wilt renew thy beauty morn by morn!
I earth in earth forget these empty courts,
And thee returning on thy silver wheels.

ALFRED, LORD TENNYSON

'The hand that signed the paper'

THE hand that signed the paper felled a city;
Five sovereign fingers taxed the breath,
Doubled the globe of dead and halved a country;
These five kings did a king to death.

The mighty hand leads to a sloping shoulder,
The finger joints are cramped with chalk;
A goose's quill has put an end to murder
That put an end to talk.

The hand that signed the treaty bred a fever,
And famine grew, and locusts came;
Great is the hand that holds dominion over
Man by a scribbled name.

The five kings count the dead but do not soften
The crusted wound nor stroke the brow:
A hand rules pity as a hand rules heaven;
Hands have no tears to flow.

DYLAN THOMAS

from *Purgatorio*

CANTO I

To run on better water now, the boat
Of my invention hoists its sails and leaves
Away to'stern that cruel stretch of sea;

And I will sing of this second kingdom
In which the human spirit cures itself
And becomes fit to leap up into heaven.

But here dead poetry rises again,
O holy Muses, since I am your own,
And here let Calliope rise a little,

Following my song with that sound from which
The pitiful Magpies felt so sharp a blow
That they despaired of ever being pardoned.

Sweet colour of oriental sapphire,
Which gathered in the clear face of the sky,
Right to the very edge of the first circle,

Restored to my eyes the touch of pleasure,
As soon as I issued from the dead air
Which had saddened my eyes and my heart.

The lovely planet which gives comfort in love
Was filling the whole eastern sky with laughter,
Hiding the Fish which followed in her train.

I turned toward the right, and fixed my mind
On the other pole, and there I saw four stars,
Never yet seen except by the first people.

The sky seemed to be glad in their sparkling:
O northern hemisphere, you are a widow
To be deprived of any sight of them!

[110]

When I had given up looking at those stars
And turned a little towards the other pole,
To where the Wain should have been, but it was gone;

I saw near me an old man, alone,
With looks deserving as much reverence
As ever any son owed to his father.

He wore his beard long and there were white strands
In it, like his hair which tumbled down
In two white bunches over his chest and shoulders;

The beams which came from those four holy lights
So played upon his face and lit it up
That I saw him as if he had been facing the sun.

'Who are you, who, going against the current
Of the blind stream, have escaped the eternal prison?'
He said, with a movement of his honoured plumage.

'Who was your guide? Whom did you have for lamp
To bring you out of the profound night
Which always darkens the infernal valley?

And are the laws of the abyss so broken?
Or has there been a change of plan in heaven,
So that, though damned, you come here to my rocks?'

My escort then took hold of me, and with
Words and touch and other indications
Made me bend knees and head in reverence.

Then he replied: 'It was not of myself
I came: a lady from heaven asked me
To help this man by bearing him company.

But since it is your will we should declare
More fully what our true condition is,
My will cannot be to say no to that.

This man has not yet seen his last evening;
But, through his madness, was so close to it
That there was hardly time to turn about.

As I have told you, I was sent to him
To rescue him; and there was no other way
Than this which I have set myself to follow.

I have shown him all the wicked people; now
I have in mind to show him all those spirits
Who cure themselves here under your care.

How I conducted him, would be a long story;
Virtue comes down from above and gives me help
In bringing him to see you and listen to you.

Now treat his coming as acceptable:
He looks for liberty, which is so loved,
As he knows who gives up his life for her.

You know this: that is why death was not bitter
To you in Utica, where you abandoned
That garment which will shine in the last day.

The eternal laws had no damage by us;
For this man is alive, I am not with Minos;
I am of the same circle as the chaste eyes

Of your Marcia, who is still to be seen praying,
O holy breast, that you will recognise her:
For her love, therefore, may you be inclined

To let us journey through your seven kingdoms:
I will convey your thanks to her, if you
Do not disdain to be mentioned in that place.'

'Marcia so pleased my eyes,' Cato replied,
'When I was still outside these present bounds,
That everything she asked of me, I did.

Now that she stays beyond the evil river,
She can move me no longer, by that law
Which was made when I issued from that place.

But if a lady from heaven moves and commands you,
As you assert, no need for flattery:
It is enough that you ask in her name.

Go therefore now, and put on him a girdle
Of simple rush, and wash his face, so that
Every trace of filth is removed from it;

For it would not do to go before
The first of the ministers of paradise
With the eyes dulled by any kind of mist.

All round about the base of this little island,
There where the waves are always beating on it,
Are rushes growing over the soft mud;

No other plant which puts out leaves and hardens
Itself, would ever live in such a place,
Because it would not give to the buffetings.

Afterwards do not come this way again;
The sun will show you, it is rising now,
A gentler way to take to climb the mountain.'

With that he disappeared; and I got up
Without a word, and went back to my escort
And turned my eyes entirely towards him.

He began: 'Follow my footsteps, let us turn
Back, for the plain slopes downwards here
Until it finishes at its lowest point.'

The dawn was conquering the morning hour
Which fled before it, so that far away
I recognised the trembling of the sea.

We went along over the lonely plain,
Like a man turning back to a road he has lost,
Who thinks he is wasting time until he finds it.

When we were at the point at which the dew
Resisted the sun, and, being on a stretch
Where there was shade, evaporated slowly,

My master gently stretched out both his hands
And touched the fine young grass; and when I saw
What his intention was, I proffered

My cheeks which were stained with tears, and there
He brought to light my natural complexion,
Which hell had hidden.

We came then to the deserted shore
Which never saw, sailing upon its waters,
Any who afterwards knew how to return.

Then he gave me the girdle another had willed for me;
And when he picked the plant of humility,
Miraculously it renewed itself at once,

Just in the very place from which he had taken it.

DANTE ALIGHIERI

To the Virgins,
To Make Much of Time

GATHER ye Rose-buds while ye may,
   Old Time is still a flying:
And this same flower that smiles today,
   Tomorrow will be dying.

The glorious Lamp of Heaven, the Sun,
   The higher he's a getting;
The sooner will his Race be run,
   And neerer he's to Setting.

That Age is best, which is the first,
   When Youth and Blood are warmer;
But being spent, the worse, and worst
   Times, still succeed the former.

Then be not coy, but use your time;
   And while ye may, goe marry:
For having lost but once your prime,
   You may for ever tarry.

ROBERT HERRICK

'Eheu fugaces'

EHEU fugaces, Postume, Postume,
Labuntur anni, nec pietas moram
   Rugis et instanti senectae
    Afferet indomitaeque morti;

Non, si trecenis quotquot eunt dies,
Amice, places illacrimabilem
   Plutona tauris: qui ter amplum
    Geryonen Tityonque tristi

Compescit unda, scilicet omnibus,
Quicumque terrae munere vescimur,
   Enaviganda, sive reges
    Sive inopes erimus coloni.

Frustra cruento Marte carebimus
Fractisque rauci fluctibus Hadriae;
   Frustra per autumnos nocentem
    Corporibus metuemus Austrum:

Visendus ater flumine languido
Cocytos errans, et Danai genus
   Infame, damnatusque longi
    Sisyphus Aeolides laboris.

Linquenda tellus, et domus, et placens
Uxor; neque harum, quas colis, arborum
   Te, praeter invisas cupressos,
    Ulla brevem dominum sequetur.

Absumet heres Caecuba dignior
Servata centum clavibus, et mero
   Tinget pavimentum superbo
    Pontificum potiore cenis.

HORACE

ALAS! Postumus, Postumus, the years glide swift away, nor will piety delay wrinkles, or impending old age, or unconquered death;

Not even, my friend, if you try with three hundred bulls a day to appease implacable Pluto, who holds three-bodied Geryon and Tityos prisoner.

By the mournful stream which must inevitably be crossed by all of us who feed on the gifts of earth, whether we are kings or poor husbandmen.

We shall escape in vain from bloody Mars and from the billows of the deep-sounding Adriatic. In vain throughout autumn shall we fear the hot south wind that injures our bodies.

We are doomed to behold black Cocytos winding in a sluggish stream, and the wicked offspring of Danaus, and Sisyphus, the son of Aeolus, condemned to endless labour.

We must leave earth, home, and loving wife. Not one of the trees which you cultivate will follow its short-lived master, except the detested cypress.

A worthier heir will consume the Caecuban which is now protected by a hundred keys, and will stain the floor with superb wine more powerful than any consumed at the dinner-parties of pontiffs.

HORACE

[117]

Ballad of the Civil Guard

THE horses are black
and black the horseshoes.
Ink stains and wax
glisten on the dark capes.
With their lead-lined skulls
they cannot weep tears.
Their souls patent leather,
they march down the roads,
hump-backed and nocturnal.
Wherever they venture,
a black rubbery hush,
a fine sand of terror.
They go where they wish,
and secrete in their skulls
a restless astronomy
of phantasmal guns.

O Gypsy City,
with flag-bedecked corners,
the moon and the pumpkin,
the bottles of cherries.
O Gypsy City,
seen once, unforgettable,
city of grief and musk,
towers of cinnamon.

At nightfall, the night
made night-black by nightfall,
in smithies, the gypsies
forge arrows and suns.
Sorely wounded, a rider
knocks at all doorways,
and cocks of glass crow

for Jerez of the Frontier.
The naked wind turns
astonishment's corner,
in the silver-black night
made night-black at nightfall.

Saints Joseph and Mary,
their castanets lost,
hunt for the gypsies
to see if they've found them.
The Virgin is dressed
in a Mayoress' robe
of chocolate wrappers,
a necklace of almonds,
and Joseph's arms move
within a silk cloak;
and Pedro Domecque
marches behind them
with three Persian sultans.
The half moon is dreaming,
an ecstatic stork,
as banners and beacons
take over flat roofs.
In the weeping mirrors
are slim-hipped dancers.
Water and shadow, water and shadow
by Jerez of the Frontier.

O Gypsy City,
with flags at the corners,
dowse your green lamps,
the Civil Guard's coming.
O Gypsy City,
once seen, unforgettable.
(Let her stay far from tides
with no combs in her hair.)

Two by two, they advance
on the city fiesta,
immortelles rustling
in bandoliers.

Two by two, they ride in,
twin nocturnes of cloth,
imagining the sky
a glass case of spurs.

The unfearing city
opens more and more doors.
Two score Civil Guards
stormed in to plunder.
All the clocks stopped
and the brandy, in bottles,
looked dead as November
to rouse no suspicion.
Prolonged screams ascended
in flight among weathervanes.
Sabres slashed breezes,
hooves trampled under.
Through the streets shadows,
old gypsies are fleeing
with half asleep horses
and jars filled with coins,
and up the steep streets,
the sinister fleeing
capes, behind them
a cyclone of scissors.

At Bethlehem Gate
the gypsies are gathered.
Saint Joseph, wounded,
shrouds a young girl.
The insistent sharp guns
clatter all the night long
as the Virgin heals infants
with the spittle of stars.
But the Civil Guard comes
and is scattering the bonfires.
Imagination,
young, naked, is seared.
Rose of the Camborios
slumps at her door, moaning,
her two breasts, sliced off,
laid there on a tray,

and other girls flee,
braids flying behind them
in air through which roses
of gunpowder burst.
When every tiled roof
was no more than a furrow,
Dawn simply shrugged
her long profile of stone.

O Gypsy City,
the Civil Guard leaves
through a tunnel of silence,
as flames ring you round.

Gypsy City, once seen,
unforgettable, let them
seek you on my brow.
Play of moon and of sand.

FEDERICO GARCÍA LORCA

Man and Wife

୬୦

TAMED by *Miltown*, we lie on Mother's bed;
the rising sun in war paint dyes us red;
in broad daylight her gilded bed-posts shine,
abandoned, almost Dionysian.
At last the trees are green on Marlborough Street,
blossoms on our magnolia ignite
the morning with their murderous five days' white.
All night I've held your hand,
as if you had
a fourth time faced the kingdom of the mad –
its hackneyed speech, its homicidal eye –
and dragged me home alive . . . Oh my *Petite*,
clearest of all God's creatures, still all air and nerve:
you were in your twenties, and I,
once hand on glass
and heart in mouth,
outdrank the Rahvs in the heat
of Greenwich Village, fainting at your feet –
too boiled and shy
and poker-faced to make a pass,
while the shrill verve
of your invective scorched the traditional South.

Now twelve years later, you turn your back.
Sleepless, you hold
your pillow to your hollows like a child;
your old-fashioned tirade –
loving, rapid, merciless –
breaks like the Atlantic Ocean on my head.

ROBERT LOWELL

[122]

The Garden

HE told me he had seen a ruined garden
Outside the town.
'Where? Where?'
I asked him quickly.
He said it lay toward the southern country;
He knew the road well: he would take me there.

Then he sat down and talked
About that garden.
He was so grandly proud and sure of it,
I listened all the evening to his talk.

And our glasses were emptied,
Talking of it.
We filled them and filled them again,
Talking of it.

He said that no one knew
The garden but himself;
Though hundreds passed it day by day,
Yet no one knew it but himself.

I

The garden, it was long and wide
And filled with great unconscious peace;
All the old trees were tall and large,
And all the birds –

The birds, he said, were like a choir
Of lively boys,
Who never went to school,
But sang instead.

He told me of the trailing flowers
Hung on the ruined walls;
The rivers and their waterfalls;
The hidden woods; the lawns; the bowers.

[123]

Small cool plantations; palm and vine,
With fig-tree growing by their side,
And violet and maidenhair
And

II

   we were late in conversation.
Talking of that most wonderful garden,
And filled our glasses again and again
Talking about that beautiful garden,

Until he vowed in the middle of drink
To lead me tomorrow to see it myself.
We closed our hands on the pact.
He vanished away through the dark.

III

Tomorrow, tomorrow, we start our walk.
Tomorrow is here and he meets me surely.
Out from the city we go and pursue
Mile after mile of the open road;

Come to a place of sudden trees,
Pass it across the fields, then on
By farmyards, through villages, over the downs:

Mile after mile we walk. He is pleased.
Our feet become heavy with dust, and we laugh,
And we talk all the while of our future delight.

IV

He came upon the garden in the dusk;
He leaned against the wall:
He pointed out its beauties in the gloom.
We lay down weary in the shadow of elms,
And stared between their branches at the moon,
And talked about tomorrow and the garden.
I knew that everything he said was true,
For we were resting up against the wall.

V

Oh hard awakening from a dream:
I thought I was in paradise.
He cooked the coffee we had brought,
Then looked about him.

We had not reached the wall, he found.
It was a little farther on.
We walked another mile or two,
And stood before the ruined gate.

He was not satisfied at all.
He said the entrance was not here.
I hardly understood his talk,
And so I watched him move about.
Indeed, it was the garden he had meant;
But not the one he had described.

VI

Then suddenly from out his conversation
I saw it in the light of his own thought:
A phantom Eden shining
Placid among his dreams.

And he, with large eyes and with hands uplifted,
Cried: 'Look, O look!' Indeed I saw the garden;
The ghostly palm and violet,
Fig, maidenhair, and fountain;

The rivers and their flowered lawns; the gleaming
Birds; and their song – I heard that clear I know.
And silent, in amazement,
We stared

Then both sat down beneath the wall and rested,
And in our conversation
Lived in the garden.

VII

'We'll come again next week,' he said at last.
'We have no leisure to explore it now;
Besides we cannot climb this crumbling wall:
Our gate is on the farther side, I know.
We'd have to go right round, and even then
I am not sure it's open till the spring.
I have affairs in town. If you don't mind,
We will go back directly. After all,
The garden cannot run away, or change.
Next week I'll have more time, and, once inside,
Who knows . . . who knows? How very curious too,
Hundreds of people pass it day by day
Along that high road over there; the cars –
Look at them! And the railway too! Well. Well,
I'm glad that no one cares for Eden now.
It would be spoilt so quickly. We'll go back
By train, if you don't mind. I've walked enough.
Look, there's the station. Eh?'

VIII

I did not see that man again
Until a year had gone or more.
I had not found him anywhere,
And many times had gone to seek
The garden, but it was not there.

One day along the country road
There was he coming all alone.
He would have passed me with a stare.
I held his arm, but he was cold,
And rudely asked me my affair.
I said, there was a garden, I'd been told . . .

IX

Then suddenly came that rapture upon us;
We saw the garden again in our mutual thought:
Blue and yellow and green,
Shining by day or by night.

[126]

'Those are the trees,' he said, 'and there is the gateway.
To-day, I think, it is open. And shall we not go there?'
Quickly we ran in our joy;
Quickly – then stopped, and stared.

X

An angel with a flaming sword
Stood large, and beautiful, and clear:
He covered up his golden eyes,
And would not look as we came near.

Birds wheeled about the flowery gate,
But we could never see inside,
Although (I often think) it stood
Slack on its hinges open wide.

The angel dropped his hopeless sword,
And stood with his great pinions furled,
And wept into his hands: but we
Feared, and turned back to our own world.

HAROLD MONRO

An Epitaph

HERE lies a most beautiful lady,
Light of step and heart was she;
I think she was the most beautiful lady
That ever was in the West Country.

But beauty vanishes; beauty passes;
However rare – rare it be;
And when I crumble, who will remember
This lady of the West Country?

WALTER DE LA MARE

The Final Word

SINCE I was ten I have not been unkind
To anyone save those who were most close:
Of my close friends one of the best is blind
One deaf, and one a priest who can't write prose.
None has a quiet mind.

Deep into night my friends with tired faces
Break language up for one word to remain,
The tall forgiving word nothing effaces,
Though without maps it travel, and explain
A pure truth in all places.

Yet death, if it should fall on us, would be
Only the smallest settling into beds:
Our last words lost because Eternity
Made its loud noise above our lifted heads
Before we ceased to see.

But, all made blind and deaf, the final word
Bequeathed by us, at the far side of
Experience, waits: there neither man nor bird
Settles, except with knowledge, or much love.
There Adam's voice is heard.

And my true love, a skylark in each eye,
Walks the small grass, and the small frightened things
Scurry to her for comfort, and can't die
While she still lives, and all the broken Kings
Kneel to her and know why.

Because she turns, her love at last expressed,
Into my arms: and then I cannot die.
I have furnished my heart to be her nest
For even if at dusk she choose to fly
Afterwards she must rest.

DOM MORAES

[129]

Christmas

A BOY was born at Bethlehem
  That knew the haunts of Galilee.
He wandered on Mount Lebanon,
  And learned to love each forest tree.

But I was born at Marlborough,
  And love the homely faces there;
And for all other men besides
  'Tis little love I have to spare.

I should not mind to die for them,
  My own dear downs, my comrades true.
But that great heart of Bethlehem,
  He died for men he never knew.

And yet, I think, at Golgotha,
  As Jesus' eyes were closed in death,
They saw with love most passionate
  The village street at Nazareth.

E. HILTON YOUNG

A Pity. We Were Such a Good Invention

THEY amputated
your thighs from my hips.
As far as I'm concerned, they're always
doctors. All of them.
They dismantled us
from each other. As far as I'm concerned,
they're engineers.
A pity. We were such a good and loving
invention: an airplane made of a man and a woman,
wings and all:
we even got off
the ground a little.
We even flew.

YEHUDA AMICHAI

'There was a small woman called G'

THERE was a small woman called G,
Who smashed two big windows at B –
They sent her to jail, her fate to bewail,
For Votes must be kept, must be kept for the male.

They asked that small woman called G,
Why she smashed those big windows at B –
She made a long speech, then made her defence,
But it wasn't no use, their heads were so dense;
They just hummed the refrain, altho' it is stale –
Votes must be kept, must be kept for the male.

They sent her to H for six months and a day,
In the coach Black Maria she went sadly away;
But she sang in this strain, as it jolted and rumbled,
We will have the Vote, we will not be humbled.
We must have the Vote by hill and by dale,
Votes shall not alone be kept for the male.

ANONYMOUS

Night Mail

(Commentary for a G.P.O. Film)

ဆ

I

THIS is the Night Mail crossing the Border,
Bringing the cheque and the postal order,

Letters for the rich, letters for the poor,
The shop at the corner, the girl next door.

Pulling up Beattock, a steady climb:
The gradient's against her, but she's on time.

Past cotton-grass and moorland boulder,
Shovelling white steam over her shoulder,

Snorting noisily, she passes
Silent miles of wind-bent grasses.

Birds turn their heads as she approaches,
Stare from bushes at her blank-faced coaches.

Sheep-dogs cannot turn her course;
They slumber on with paws across.

In the farm she passes no one wakes,
But a jug in a bedroom gently shakes.

II

Dawn freshens. Her climb is done.
Down towards Glasgow she descends,
Towards the steam tugs yelping down a glade of cranes,
Towards the fields of apparatus, the furnaces
Set on the dark plain like gigantic chessmen.
All Scotland waits for her:
In dark glens, beside pale-green lochs,
Men long for news.

III

Letters of thanks, letters from banks,
Letters of joy from girl and boy,
Receipted bills and invitations
To inspect new stock or to visit relations,
And applications for situations,
And timid lovers' declarations,
And gossip, gossip from all the nations,
News circumstantial, news financial,
Letters with holiday snaps to enlarge in,
Letters with faces scrawled on the margin,
Letters from uncles, cousins and aunts,
Letters to Scotland from the South of France,
Letters of condolence to Highlands and Lowlands,
Written on paper of every hue,
The pink, the violet, the white and the blue,
The chatty, the catty, the boring, the adoring,
The cold and official and the heart's outpouring,
Clever, stupid, short and long,
The typed and the printed and the spelt all wrong.

IV

Thousands are still asleep,
Dreaming of terrifying monsters
Or a friendly tea beside the band in Cranston's or Crawford's:
Asleep in working Glasgow, asleep in well-set Edinburgh,
Asleep in granite Aberdeen,
They continue their dreams,
But shall wake soon and hope for letters,
And none will hear the postman's knock
Without a quickening of the heart.
For who can bear to feel himself forgotten?

W.H. AUDEN

Remembrance

ನ೧೨

Cold in the earth, and the deep snow piled above thee!
Far, far removed, cold in the dreary grave!
Have I forgot, my Only Love, to love thee,
Severed at last by Time's all-wearing wave?

Now, when alone, do my thoughts no longer hover
Over the mountains on Angora's shore;
Resting their wings where heath and fern-leaves cover
That noble heart for ever, ever more?

Cold in the earth, and fifteen wild Decembers
From those brown hills have melted into spring –
Faithful indeed is the spirit that remembers
After such years of change and suffering!

Sweet Love of youth, forgive if I forget thee
While the World's tide is bearing me along:
Sterner desires and darker hopes beset me,
Hopes which obscure but cannot do thee wrong.

No other Sun has lightened up my heaven;
No other Star has ever shone for me;
All my life's bliss from thy dear life was given –
All my life's bliss is in the grave with thee.

But when the days of golden dreams had perished
And even Despair was powerless to destroy,
Then did I learn how existence could be cherished,
Strengthened and fed without the aid of joy;

Then did I check the tears of useless passion,
Weaned my young soul from yearning after thine;
Sternly denied its burning wish to hasten
Down to that tomb already more than mine!

And even yet, I dare not let it languish,
Dare not indulge in Memory's rapturous pain;
Once drinking deep of that divinest anguish,
How could I seek the empty world again?

Emily Brontë

The Rolling English Road

BEFORE the Roman came to Rye or out to Severn strode,
The rolling English drunkard made the rolling English road.
A reeling road, a rolling road, that rambles round the shire,
And after him the parson ran, the sexton and the squire;
A merry road, a mazy road, and such as we did tread
The night we went to Birmingham by way of Beachy Head.

I knew no harm of Bonaparte and plenty of the Squire,
And for to fight the Frenchman I did not much desire;
But I did bash their waggonets because they came arrayed
To straighten out the crooked road an English drunkard made,
Where you and I went down the lane with ale-mugs in our hands,
The night we went to Glastonbury by way of Goodwin Sands.

His sins they were forgiven him; or why do flowers run
Behind him, and the hedges all strengthening in the sun?
The wild thing went from left to right and knew not which was
        which,
But the wild rose was above him when they found him in the ditch.
God pardon us, nor harden us; we did not see so clear
The night we went to Bannockburn by way of Brighton Pier.

My friends, we will not go again or ape an ancient rage,
Or stretch the folly of our youth to be the shame of age,
But walk with clearer eyes and ears this path that wandereth,
And see undrugged in evening light the decent inn of death;
For there is good news yet to hear and fine things to be seen,
Before we go to Paradise by way of Kensal Green.

G.K. CHESTERTON

I Am

৵৽

I AM: yet what I am none cares or knows,
   My friends forsake me like a memory lost,
I am the self-consumer of my woes,
   They rise and vanish in oblivious host,
Like shades in love and death's oblivion lost;
And yet I am, and live with shadows tost

Into the nothingness of scorn and noise,
   Into the living sea of waking dreams,
Where there is neither sense of life nor joys,
   But the vast shipwreck of my life's esteems;
And e'en the dearest – that I loved the best –
Are strange – nay, rather stranger than the rest.

I long for scenes where man has never trod;
   A place where woman never smiled or wept;
There to abide with my Creator, GOD,
   And sleep as I in childhood sweetly slept:
Untroubling and untroubled where I lie;
The grass below – above the vaulted sky.

JOHN CLARE

My Lover

❧

For I will consider my lover, who shall remain nameless.

For at the age of 49 he can make the noise of five different kinds of
    lorry changing gear on a hill.

For he sometimes does this on the stairs at his place of work.

For he is embarrassed when people overhear him.

For he can also imitate at least three different kinds of train.

For these include the London tube train, the steam engine, and the
    Southern Rail electric.

For he supports Tottenham Hotspur with joyful and unswerving
    devotion.

For he abhors Arsenal, whose supporters are uncivilized and rough.

For he explains that Spurs are magic, whereas Arsenal are boring and
    defensive.

For I knew nothing of this six months ago, nor did I want to.

For now it all enchants me.

For this he performs in ten degrees.

For first he presents himself as a nice, serious, liberated person.

For secondly he sits through many lunches, discussing life and love and
    never mentioning football.

For thirdly he is careful not to reveal how much he dislikes losing an
    argument.

For fourthly he talks about the women in his past, acknowledging that
    some of it must have been his fault.

For fifthly he is so obviously reasonable that you are inclined to doubt
    this.

For sixthly he invites himself round for a drink one evening.

For seventhly you consume two bottles of wine between you.

For eighthly he stays the night.

For ninthly you cannot wait to see him again.

For tenthly he does not get in touch for several days.

For having achieved his object he turns again to his other interests.

For he will not miss his evening class or his choir practice for a
    woman.

For he is out nearly all the time.

For you cannot even get him on the telephone.

For he is the kind of man who has been driving women round the
    bend for generations.

For, sad to say, this thought does not bring you to your senses.

For he is charming.

For he is good with animals and children.

For his voice is both reassuring and sexy.

For he drives an A-registration Vauxhall Astra estate.

For he goes at 80 miles per hour on the motorways.

For when I plead with him he says, 'I'm not going any slower than
    this.'

For he is convinced he knows his way around better than anyone else
    on earth.

For he does not encourage suggestions from his passengers.

For if he ever got lost there would be hell to pay.

For he sometimes makes me sleep on the wrong side of my own bed.

For he cannot be bossed around.

For he has this grace, that he is happy to eat fish fingers or Chinese
    takeaway or to cook the supper himself.

For he knows about my cooking and is realistic.

For he makes me smooth cocoa with bubbles on the top.

For he drinks and smokes at least as much as I do.

For he is obsessed with sex.

For he would never say it is overrated.

For he grew up before the permissive society and remembers his
    adolescence.

For he does not insist it is healthy and natural, nor does he ask me
    what I would like him to do.

For he has a few ideas of his own.

For he has never been able to sleep much and talks with me late
    into the night.

For we wear each other out with our wakefulness.

For he makes me feel like a light-bulb that cannot switch itself off.
For he inspires poem after poem.
For he is clean and tidy but not too concerned with his appearance.
For he lets the barber cut his hair too short and goes round looking
    like a convict for a fortnight.
For when I ask if this necklace is all right he replies, 'Yes, if no means
    looking at three others.'
For he was shocked when younger team-mates began using talcum
    powder in the changing-room.
For his old-fashioned masculinity is the cause of continual merriment
    on my part.
For this puzzles him.

WENDY COPE

Wild Women Blues

I'VE got a different system
And a way of my own,
When my man starts kicking
I let him find another home.
I get full of good liquor
And walk the street all night,
Go home and put my man out
If he don't treat me right,
Wild women don't worry,
Wild women don't have the blues.

You never get nothing
By being an angel child,
You better change your ways
And get real wild.
I want to tell you something
I wouldn't tell you no lie,
Wild women are the only kind
That really get by,
'Cause wild women don't worry,
Wild women don't have the blues.

IDA COX

[141]

'it may not always be so'

it may not always be so;and i say
that if your lips,which i have loved,should touch
another's,and your dear strong fingers clutch
his heart,as mine in time not far away;
if on another's face your sweet hair lay
in such a silence as i know,or such
great writhing words as,uttering overmuch,
stand helplessly before the spirit at bay;

if this should be,i say if this should be –
you of my heart,send me a little word;
that i may go unto him,and take his hands,
saying,Accept all happiness from me.
Then shall i turn my face,and hear one bird
sing terribly afar in the lost lands.

E.E. CUMMINGS

Leisure

WHAT is this life if, full of care,
We have no time to stand and stare?

No time to stand beneath the boughs
And stare as long as sheep or cows.

No time to see, when woods we pass,
Where squirrels hide their nuts in grass.

No time to see, in broad daylight,
Streams full of stars, like skies at night.

No time to turn at Beauty's glance,
And watch her feet, how they can dance.

No time to wait till her mouth can
Enrich that smile her eyes began.

A poor life this if, full of care,
We have no time to stand and stare.

W.H. DAVIES

The Crowning of Dreaming John

I

SEVEN days he travelled
Down the roads of England,
Out of leafy Warwick lanes
Into London Town.
Grey and very wrinkled
Was Dreaming John of Grafton,
But seven days he walked to see
A king put on his crown.

Down the streets of London
He asked the crowded people
Where would be the crowning
And when would it begin.
He said he'd got a shilling,
A shining silver shilling,
But when he came to Westminster
They wouldn't let him in.

Dreaming John of Grafton
Looked upon the people,
Laughed a little laugh, and then
Whistled and was gone.
Out along the long roads,
The twisting roads of England,
Back into the Warwick lanes
Wandered Dreaming John.

II

As twilight touched with her ghostly fingers
All the meadows and mellow hills,
And the great sun swept in his robes of glory –

Woven of petals of daffodils
And jewelled and fringed with leaves of the roses –
Down the plains of the western way,
Among the rows of the scented clover
Dreaming John in his dreaming lay.

Since dawn had folded the stars of heaven
He'd counted a score of miles and five
And now, with a vagabond heart untroubled
And proud as the properest man alive,
He sat him down with a limber spirit
That all men covet and few may keep,
And he watched the summer draw round her beauty
The shadow that shepherds the world to sleep.

And up from the valleys and shining rivers,
And out of the shadowy wood-ways wild,
And down from the secret hills, and streaming
Out of the shimmering undefiled
Wonder of sky that arched him over,
Came a company shod in gold
And girt in gowns of a thousand blossoms,
Laughing and rainbow-aureoled.

Wrinkled and grey and with eyes a-wonder
And soul beatified, Dreaming John
Watched the marvellous company gather
While over the clover a glory shone;
They bore on their brows the hues of heaven,
Their limbs were sweet with flowers of the fields,
And their feet were bright with the gleaming treasure
That prodigal earth to her children yields.

They stood before him, and John was laughing
As they were laughing; he knew them all,
Spirits of trees and pools and meadows,
Mountain and windy waterfall,
Spirits of clouds and skies and rivers,
Leaves and shadows and rain and sun,
A crowded, jostling, laughing army,
And Dreaming John knew every one.

Among them then was a sound of singing
And chiming music, as one came down
The level rows of the scented clover,
Bearing aloft a flashing crown;
No word of a man's desert was spoken,
Nor any word of a man's unworth,
But there on the wrinkled brow it rested,
And Dreaming John was king of the earth.

III

Dreaming John of Grafton
Went away to London,
Saw the coloured banners fly,
Heard the great bells ring,
But though his tongue was civil
And he had a silver shilling,
They wouldn't let him in to see
The crowning of the King.

So back along the long roads,
The leafy roads of England,
Dreaming John went carolling,
Travelling alone,
And in a summer evening,
Among the scented clover,
He held before a shouting throng
A crowning of his own.

JOHN DRINKWATER

On Monsieur's Departure

I GRIEVE and dare not show my discontent,
I love and yet am forced to seem to hate,
I do, yet dare not say I ever meant,
I seem stark mute but inwardly do prate.
   I am and not, I freeze and yet am burned,
   Since from myself another self I turned.

My care is like my shadow in the sun,
Follows me flying, flies when I pursue it,
Stands and lies by me, doth what I have done.
His too familiar care doth make me rue it.
   No means I find to rid him from my breast,
   Till by the end of things it be supprest.

Some gentler passion slide into my mind,
For I am soft and made of melting snow;
Or be more cruel, love, and so be kind.
Let me or float or sink, be high or low.
   Or let me live with some more sweet content.
   Or die and so forget what love ere meant.

ELIZABETH I

Adam Pos'd

Cou'd our first father, at his toilsome plough,
Thorns in his path, and labour on his brow,
Cloath'd only in a rude, unpolish'd skin,
Cou'd he a vain fantastick nymph have seen,
In all her airs, in all her antick graces,
Her various fashions, and more various faces;
How had it pos'd that skill, which late assign'd
Just appellations to each several kind!
A right idea of the sight to frame;
T'have guest from what new element she came;
T'have hit the wav'ring form, and giv'n this Thing a name.

ANNE FINCH, COUNTESS OF WINCHILSEA

The Golden Journey to Samarkand

Prologue

I

WE who with songs beguile your pilgrimage
  And swear that Beauty lives though lilies die,
We Poets of the proud old lineage
  Who sing to find your hearts, we know not why, –

What shall we tell you? Tales, marvellous tales
  Of ships and stars and isles where good men rest,
Where nevermore the rose of sunset pales,
  And winds and shadows fall toward the West:

And there the world's first huge white-bearded kings
  In dim glades sleeping, murmur in their sleep,
And closer round their breasts the ivy clings,
  Cutting its pathway slow and red and deep.

II

And how beguile you? Death has no repose
  Warmer and deeper than that Orient sand
Which hides the beauty and bright faith of those
  Who made the Golden Journey to Samarkand.

And now they wait and whiten peaceably,
  Those conquerors, those poets, those so fair:
They know time comes, not only you and I,
  But the whole world shall whiten, here or there;

When those long caravans that cross the plain
  With dauntless feet and sound of silver bells
Put forth no more for glory or for gain,
  Take no more solace from the palm-girt wells.

When the great markets by the sea shut fast
　　All that calm Sunday that goes on and on:
When even lovers find their peace at last,
　　And Earth is but a star, that once had shone.

Epilogue
At the Gate of the Sun, Bagdad, in olden time

THE MERCHANTS (*together*)
Away, for we are ready to a man!
　　Our camels sniff the evening and are glad.
Lead on, O Master of the Caravan:
　　Lead on the Merchant-Princes of Bagdad.

THE CHIEF DRAPER
Have we not Indian carpets dark as wine,
　　Turbans and sashes, gowns and bows and veils,
And broideries of intricate design,
　　And printed hangings in enormous bales?

THE CHIEF GROCER
We have rose-candy, we have spikenard,
　　Mastic and terebinth and oil and spice,
And such sweet jams meticulously jarred
　　As God's own Prophet eats in Paradise.

THE PRINCIPAL JEWS
And we have manuscripts in peacock styles
　　By Ali of Damascus; we have swords
Engraved with storks and apes and crocodiles,
　　And heavy beaten necklaces, for Lords.

THE MASTER OF THE CARAVAN
But you are nothing but a lot of Jews.

THE PRINCIPAL JEWS
Sir, even dogs have daylight, and we pay.

THE MASTER OF THE CARAVAN
But who are ye in rags and rotten shoes,
　　You dirty-bearded, blocking up the way?

[150]

THE PILGRIMS

We are the Pilgrims, master; we shall go
    Always a little further: it may be
Beyond that last blue mountain barred with snow,
    Across that angry or that glimmering sea,

White on a throne or guarded in a cave
    There lives a prophet who can understand
Why men were born: but surely we are brave,
    Who make the Golden Journey to Samarkand.

THE CHIEF MERCHANT

We gnaw the nail of hurry. Master, away!

ONE OF THE WOMEN

O turn your eyes to where your children stand.
Is not Bagdad the beautiful? O stay!

THE MERCHANTS (*in chorus*)

We take the Golden Road to Samarkand.

AN OLD MAN

Have you not girls and garlands in your homes,
    Eunuchs and Syrian boys at your command?
Seek not excess: God hateth him who roams!

THE MERCHANTS (*in chorus*)

We make the Golden Journey to Samarkand.

A PILGRIM WITH A BEAUTIFUL VOICE

Sweet to ride forth at evening from the wells
    When shadows pass gigantic on the sand,
And softly through the silence beat the bells
    Along the Golden Road to Samarkand.

A MERCHANT

We travel not for trafficking alone:
    By hotter winds our fiery hearts are fanned:
For lust of knowing what should not be known
    We make the Golden Journey to Samarkand.

[151]

THE MASTER OF THE CARAVAN
Open the gate, O watchman of the night!

THE WATCHMAN
Ho, travellers, I open. For what land
Leave you the dim-moon city of delight?

THE MERCHANTS (*with a shout*)
We make the Golden Journey to Samarkand.

(*The Caravan passes through the gate.*)

THE WATCHMAN (*consoling the women*)
What would ye, ladies? It was ever thus.
　Men are unwise and curiously planned.

A WOMAN
They have their dreams, and do not think of us.

VOICES OF THE CARAVAN (*in the distance, singing*)
We make the Golden Journey to Samarkand.

JAMES ELROY FLECKER

Villanelle

ನಾ

Veering towards midday we soon lose speed,
Conviction fails in movements we've rehearsed.
The concentration's lacking, not the need.

The lies we tell can never supersede
A conscious doubt which aggravates our thirst.
Veering towards midday we soon lose speed.

Distracted while experiments proceed,
The charms all crack, the glass containers burst.
The concentration's lacking, not the need.

Somehow it's two o'clock and then we're freed –
The afternoons of failure are the worst.
Veering towards midday we soon lose speed.

The gold sun waits. – When nothing would impede
Our progress to the moment, we're immersed.
The concentration's lacking, not the need.

A newer Icarus might yet succeed
Who has a sense of knowing what goes first.
Veering towards midday we soon lose speed.
The concentration's lacking, not the need.

HARRY GUEST

Afterwards

ನುಲ

WHEN the Present has latched its postern behind my tremulous stay,
   And the May month flaps its glad green leaves like wings,
Delicate-filmed as new-spun silk, will the neighbours say,
   'He was a man who used to notice such things'?

If it be in the dusk when, like an eyelid's soundless blink,
   The dewfall-hawk comes crossing the shades to alight
Upon the wind-warped upland thorn, a gazer may think,
   'To him this must have been a familiar sight.'

If I pass during some nocturnal blackness, mothy and warm,
   When the hedgehog travels furtively over the lawn,
One may say, 'He strove that such innocent creatures should come to
    no harm,
   But he could do little for them; and now he is gone.'

If, when hearing that I have been stilled at last, they stand at the door
   Watching the full-starred heavens that winter sees,
Will this thought rise on those who will meet my face no more,
   'He was one who had an eye for such mysteries'?

And will any say when my bell of quittance is heard in the gloom,
   And a crossing breeze cuts a pause in its outrollings,
Till they rise again, as they were a new bell's boom,
   'He hears it not now, but used to notice such things'?

THOMAS HARDY

I remember, I remember

I REMEMBER, I remember
  The house where I was born,
The little window where the sun
  Came peeping in at morn;
He never came a wink too soon
  Nor brought too long a day;
But now, I often wish the night
  Had borne my breath away.

I remember, I remember
  The roses, red and white,
The violets, and the lily-cups –
  Those flowers made of light!
The lilacs where the robin built,
  And where my brother set
The laburnum on his birth-day, –
  The tree is living yet!

I remember, I remember
  Where I was used to swing,
And thought the air must rush as fresh
  To swallows on the wing;
My spirit flew in feathers then
  That is so heavy now,
And summer pools could hardly cool
  The fever on my brow.

I remember, I remember
  The fir trees dark and high;
I used to think their slender tops
  Were close against the sky:
It was a childish ignorance,
  But now 'tis little joy
To know I'm farther off from Heaven
  Than when I was a boy.

THOMAS HOOD

Coming Round

I COULD be alone in a garden
lulled by all the official signs of peace: tactful birds, obsequious breeze,
the pool licking at its marble cup, the lawn's velvet nap
    flowing beneath attendant trees;
a single cloud shaped like a Maxim gun.
Beyond the gate, servants circle endlessly,
distant bodies orbiting a famous sun;
mounted on great black bikes they pedal wildly for the chance
of being first down, padding up to the gate in the thick sandals
they carve from worn-out tyres, to press a face to the bars:
houseboys, garden boys, butcher boys, office boys, ice cream boys
swerving by on threadbare rubber treads like dodgem cars.

The still blue water touching placid lip to tiled step
suggests one way at least of staying cool
if only I will take the plunge . . .
Now I'm alone in a garden in a swimming pool
keeping my head down, dazed by terrible dreams:
ground glass in the salt-cellars, a greenish cast to the morning milk,
someone's watch-dog, a brute with a mallet head, strangled before he
    could bark,
garden forks with cunningly razored tines,
persistent reports that certain prams have been fingered in the park,
the embarrassing urge to pray
in public. There must be sensible ways of reading the signs
and boys will be boys, they say.

The sun's forever signalling for attention, brassy heat like a bugle blast;
too happy for Taps, and far too late for Reveille.
I'm up to my neck and tiring fast
in glass blue water seeming to harden against every stroke
but I press on aiming to swim into focus soon. The eyes
at the gate note precisely how often I stop to choke
back water. Swimming is difficult – arm, breathe, kick, arm . . .
this game I feel could take the skin off a man;
bone tested against glass wins a small shriek. I know where I am now,
knowing how much easier it would be simply to drown.
I am alone in a garden in a swimming pool in white South Africa,
turning brown.

CHRISTOPHER HOPE

Battle-Hymn of the Republic

MINE eyes have seen the glory of the coming of the Lord:
He is trampling out the vintage where the grapes of wrath are stored;
He hath loosed the fateful lightning of His terrible swift sword;
　　　His truth is marching on.

I have seen Him in the watch-fires of a hundred circling camps;
They have builded Him an altar in the evening dews and damps;
I can read His righteous sentence by the dim and flaring lamps:
　　　His day is marching on.

I have read a fiery gospel writ in burnished rows of steel:
'As ye deal with my contemners, so with you my grace shall deal;
Let the Hero, born of woman, crush the serpent with his heel,
　　　Since God is marching on.'

He has sounded forth the trumpet that shall never call retreat;
He is sifting out the hearts of men before His judgment-seat;
Oh, be swift, my soul, to answer Him! be jubilant, my feet!
　　　Our God is marching on.

In the beauty of the lilies Christ was born across the sea,
With a glory in his bosom that transfigures you and me:
As he died to make men holy, let us die to make men free,
　　　While God is marching on.

JULIA WARD HOWE

The Dong with a Luminous Nose

WHEN awful darkness and silence reign
Over the great Gromboolian plain,
   Through the long, long wintry nights;
When the angry breakers roar
As they beat on the rocky shore;
   When storm-clouds brood on the towering heights
Of the hills of the Chankly Bore:
Then, through the vast and gloomy dark,
There moves what seems a fiery spark,
   A lonely spark with silvery rays
   Piercing the coal-black night,
   A meteor strange and bright:
Hither and thither the vision strays,
   A single lurid light.

Slowly it wanders, – pauses, – creeps,
Anon it sparkles, – flashes and leaps;
And ever as onward it gleaming goes
A light on the Bong-tree stems it throws.
And those who watch at that midnight hour
From hall or terrace, or lofty tower,
Cry, as the wild light passes along,
    'The Dong! – the Dong!
   The wandering Dong through the forest goes!
    The Dong! the Dong!
   The Dong with a luminous Nose!'

    Long years ago
   The Dong was happy and gay,
Till he fell in love with a Jumbly Girl
   Who came to those shores one day,
For the Jumblies came in a sieve, they did,
Landing at eve near the Zemmery Fidd
    Where the Oblong Oysters grow,
   And the rocks are smooth and gray.
And all the woods and the valleys rang
With the Chorus they daily and nightly sang,

'Far and few, far and few,
Are the lands where the Jumblies live;
Their heads are green, and their hands are blue
And they went to sea in a sieve.'

Happily, happily passed those days!
    While the cheerful Jumblies stayed;
  They danced in circlets all night long,
  To the plaintive pipe of the lively Dong,
    In moonlight, shine, or shade.
For day and night he was always there
By the side of the Jumbly Girl so fair,
With her sky-blue hands, and her sea-green hair.
Till the morning came of that hateful day
When the Jumblies sailed in their sieve away,
And the Dong was left on the cruel shore
Gazing – gazing for evermore,
Ever keeping his weary eyes on
That pea-green sail on the far horizon,
Singing the Jumbly Chorus still
As he sate all day on the grassy hill,
    'Far and few, far and few,
    Are the lands where the Jumblies live;
    Their heads are green, and their hands are blue,
    And they went to sea in a sieve.'

But when the sun was low in the West,
    The Dong arose and said:
'What little sense I once possessed
    Has quite gone out of my head!'
And since that day he wanders still
By lake and forest, marsh and hill,
Singing – 'O somewhere, in valley or plain
Might I find my Jumbly Girl again!
For ever I'll seek by lake and shore
Till I find my Jumbly Girl once more!'

    Playing a pipe with silvery squeaks,
    Since then his Jumbly Girl he seeks,
    And because by night he could not see,
    He gathered the bark of the Twangum Tree
        On the flowery plain that grows.

And he wove him a wondrous Nose,
A Nose as strange as a Nose could be!
Of vast proportions and painted red,
And tied with cords to the back of his head.
In a hollow rounded space it ended
With a luminous Lamp within suspended,
All fenced about
With a bandage stout
To prevent the wind from blowing it out;
And with holes all round to send the light
In gleaming rays on the dismal night.

And now each night, and all night long,
Over those plains still roams the Dong;
And above the wail of the Chimp and Snipe
You may hear the squeak of his plaintive pipe
While ever he seeks, but seeks in vain
To meet with his Jumbly Girl again;
Lonely and wild – all night he goes,
The Dong with a luminous Nose!
And all who watch at the midnight hour,
From hall or terrace, or lofty tower,
Cry, as they trace the meteor bright,
Moving along through the dreary night,
'This is the hour when forth he goes,
The Dong with a luminous Nose!
Yonder – over the plain he goes;
He goes!
He goes;
The Dong with a luminous Nose!'

EDWARD LEAR

The Passionate Shepherd to his Love

ౚ

COME live with me, and be my love,
And we will all the pleasures prove,
That valleys, groves, hills and fields,
Woods, or steepy mountain yields,

And we will sit upon the rocks,
Seeing the shepherds feed their flocks
By shallow rivers, to whose falls
Melodious birds sing madrigals.

And I will make thee beds of roses,
And a thousand fragrant posies,
A cap of flowers and a kirtle
Embroidered all with leaves of myrtle,

A gown made of the finest wool
Which from our pretty lambs we pull,
Fair lined slippers for the cold,
With buckles of the purest gold;

A belt of straw and ivy-buds,
With coral clasps and amber studs,
And if these pleasures may thee move,
Come live with me, and be my love.

The shepherd swains shall dance and sing
For thy delight each May-morning,
If these delights thy mind may move;
Then live with me, and be my love.

CHRISTOPHER MARLOWE

The Definition of Love

My Love is of a birth as rare
As 'tis for object strange and high:
It was begotten by Despair
Upon Impossibility.

Magnanimous Despair alone
Could show me so divine a thing,
Where feeble Hope could ne'r have flown
But vainly flapt its Tinsel Wing.

And yet I quickly might arrive
Where my extended Soul is fixt,
But Fate does Iron wedges drive,
And alwaies crouds it self betwixt.

For Fate with jealous Eye does see
Two perfect Loves; nor lets them close:
Their union would her ruine be,
And her Tyrannick pow'r depose.

And therefore her Decrees of Steel
Us as the distant Poles have plac'd,
(Though Loves whole World on us doth wheel)
Not by themselves to be embrac'd.

Unless the giddy Heaven fall,
And Earth some new Convulsion tear;
And, us to joyn, the World should all
Be cramp'd into a *Planisphere*.

As Lines so Loves *oblique* may well
Themselves in every Angle greet:
But ours so truly *Paralel*,
Though infinite can never meet.

Therefore the Love which us doth bind,
But Fate so enviously debarrs,
Is the conjunction of the Mind,
And Opposition of the Stars.

ANDREW MARVELL

[163]

Cargoes

Quinquereme of Nineveh from distant Ophir
Rowing home to haven in sunny Palestine
With a cargo of ivory,
And apes and peacocks,
Sandalwood, cedarwood, and sweet white wine.

Stately Spanish galleon coming from the Isthmus,
Dipping through the Tropics by the palm-green shores.
With a cargo of diamonds,
Emeralds, amethysts,
Topazes, and cinnamon, and gold moidores.

Dirty British coaster with a salt-caked smoke stack
Butting through the Channel in the mad March days,
With a cargo of Tyne coal,
Road-rail, pig-lead,
Firewood, iron-ware, and cheap tin trays.

JOHN MASEFIELD

Let Me Die a Youngman's Death

LET me die a youngman's death
not a clean & inbetween
the sheets holywater death
not a famous-last-words
peaceful out of breath death

When I'm 73
& in constant good tumour
may I be mown down at dawn
by a bright red sports car
on my way home
from an allnight party

Or when I'm 91
with silver hair
& sitting in a barber's chair
may rival gangsters
with hamfisted tommyguns burst in
& give me a short back & insides

Or when I'm 104
& banned from the Cavern
may my mistress
catching me in bed with her daughter
& fearing for her son
cut me up into little pieces
& throw away every piece but one

Let me die a youngman's death
not a free from sin tiptoe in
candle wax & waning death
not a curtains drawn by angels borne
'what a nice way to go' death

ROGER McGOUGH

Maternity

ONE wept whose only child was dead,
  New-born, ten years ago.
'Weep not; he is in bliss,' they said.
  She answered, 'Even so,

'Ten years ago was born in pain
  A child, not now forlorn.
But oh, ten years ago, in vain,
  A mother, a mother was born.'

ALICE MEYNELL

I'm Explaining a Few Things

YOU are going to ask: and where are the lilacs?
and the poppy-petalled metaphysics?
and the rain repeatedly spattering
its words and drilling them full
of apertures and birds?

I'll tell you all the news.

I lived in a suburb,
a suburb of Madrid, with bells,
and clocks, and trees.

From there you could look out
Over Castille's dry face:
a leather ocean.
                    My house was called
the house of flowers, because in every cranny
geraniums burst: it was
a good-looking house
with its dogs and children.
                    Remember, Raúl?
Eh, Rafael?
                    Federico, do you remember
from under the ground
my balconies on which
the light of June drowned flowers in your mouth?
                              Brother, my brother!
Everything
loud with big voices, the salt of merchandises,
pile-ups of palpitating bread,
the stalls of my suburb of Argüelles with its statue
like a drained inkwell in a swirl of hake:
oil flowed into spoons.

a deep baying
of feet and hands swelled in the streets,
metres, litres, the sharp
measure of life,
                    stacked-up fish,
the texture of roofs with a cold sun in which
the weather vane falters,
the fine, frenzied ivory of potatoes,
wave on wave of tomatoes rolling down to the sea.

And one morning all that was burning,
one morning the bonfires
leapt out of the earth
devouring human beings –
and from then on fire,
gunpowder from then on,
and from then on blood.
Bandits with planes and Moors,
bandits with finger-rings and duchesses,
bandits with black friars spattering blessings
came through the sky to kill children
and the blood of children ran through the streets
without fuss, like children's blood.

Jackals that the jackals would despise,
stones that the dry thistle would bite on and spit out,
vipers that the vipers would abominate!

Face to face with you I have seen the blood
of Spain tower like a tide
to drown you in one wave
of pride and knives!

Treacherous
generals:
see my dead house,
look at broken Spain:
from every house burning metal flows
instead of flowers,
from every socket of Spain
Spain emerges
and from every dead child a rifle with eyes,

and from every crime bullets are born
which will one day find
the bull's eye of your hearts.

And you will ask: why doesn't his poetry
speak of dreams and leaves
and the great volcanoes of his native land?

Come and see the blood in the streets.
Come and see
the blood in the streets.
Come and see the blood
in the streets!

PABLO NERUDA

A Considered Reply to a Child

'I LOVE you', you said between two mouthfuls of pudding.
But not funny; I didn't want to laugh at all.
Rolling three years' experience in a ball,
You nudged it friendlily across the table.

A stranger, almost, I was flattered – no kidding.
It's not every day I hear a thing like that;
And when I do my answer's never pat.
I'm about nine times your age, ten times less able

To say – what you said; incapable of unloading
Plonk at someone's feet, like a box of bricks,
A declaration. When I try, it sticks
Like fish-bones in my throat; my eyes tingle.

What's called 'passion', you'll learn, may become 'overriding'.
But not in me it doesn't: I'm that smart,
I can give everything and keep my heart.
Kisses are kisses. No need for souls to mingle.

Bed's bed, what's more, and you'd say it's meant for sleeping;
And, believe me, you'd be absolutely right.
With luck you'll never lie awake all night,
Someone beside you (rather like 'crying') weeping.

JONATHAN PRICE

[170]

The Lie

Go, soul, the body's guest,
  Upon a thankless arrant;
Fear not to touch the best;
  The truth shall be thy warrant.
    Go, since I needs must die,
    And give the world the lie.

Say to the court, it glows
  And shines like rotten wood;
Say to the church, it shows
  What's good, and doth no good:
    If church and court reply,
    Then give them both the lie.

Tell potentates, they live
  Acting by others' action,
Not loved unless they give,
  Not strong but by affection.
    If potentates reply,
    Give potentates the lie.

SIR WALTER RALEGH

The Second Wife

SHE knows, being woman, that for him she holds
The space kept for the second blossoming,
Unmixed with dreams, held tightly in the folds
Of the accepted and long-proper thing –
She, duly loved; and he, proud of her looks
Shy of her wit. And of that other she knows
She had a slim throat, a nice taste in books,
And grew petunias in squat garden rows.
Thus knowing all, she feels both safe and strange;
Safe in his life, of which she has a share;
Safe in her undisturbed, cool, equal place,
In the sweet commonness that will not change;
And strange, when, at the door, in the spring air,
She hears him sigh, old Aprils in his face.

LIZETTE WOODWORTH REESE

The Choice

Think thou and act; tomorrow thou shalt die.
   Outstretch'd in the sun's warmth upon the shore,
   Thou say'st: 'Man's measured path is all gone o'er:
Up all his years, steeply, with strain and sigh,
Man clomb until he touch'd the truth; and I,
   Even I, am he whom it was destined for.'
   How should this be? Art thou then so much more
Than they who sow'd, that thou shouldst reap thereby?

Nay, come up hither. From this wave-wash'd mound
   Unto the furthest flood-brim look with me;
Then reach on with thy thought till it be drown'd.
   Miles and miles distant though the last line be,
And though thy soul sail leagues and leagues beyond, –
   Still, leagues beyond those leagues, there is more sea.

DANTE GABRIEL ROSSETTI

Attack

From a note in my diary while observing the
Hindenburg Line attack.

━━━━━━━━━━

AT dawn the ridge emerges massed and dun
In the wild purple of the glow'ring sun,
Smouldering through spouts of drifting smoke that shroud
The menacing scarred slope; and, one by one,
Tanks creep and topple forward to the wire.
The barrage roars and lifts. Then, clumsily bowed
With bombs and guns and shovels and battle-gear,
Men jostle and climb to meet the bristling fire.
Lines of grey, muttering faces, masked with fear,
They leave their trenches, going over the top,
While time ticks blank and busy on their wrists,
And hope, with furtive eyes and grappling fists,
Flounders in mud. O Jesu, make it stop!

SIEGFRIED SASSOON

from *If I Should Ever by Chance*

IF I should ever by chance grow rich
I'll buy Codham, Cockridden, and Childerditch,
Roses, Pyrgo, and Lapwater,
And let them all to my elder daughter.
The rent I shall ask of her will be only
Each year's first violets, white and lonely,
The first primroses and orchises –
She must find them before I do, that is.
But if she finds a blossom on furze
Without rent they shall all for ever be hers,
Whenever I am sufficiently rich:
Codham, Cockridden, and Childerditch,
Roses, Pyrgo, and Lapwater, –
I shall give them all to my elder daughter.

EDWARD THOMAS

Tichborne's Elegy

My prime of youth is but a frost of cares,
My feast of joy is but a dish of pain,
My crop of corn is but a field of tares,
And all my good is but vain hope of gain;
The day is past, and yet I saw no sun,
And now I live, and now my life is done.

My tale was heard and yet it was not told,
My fruit is fallen and yet my leaves are green,
My youth is spent and yet I am not old,
I saw the world and yet I was not seen;
My thread is cut and yet it is not spun,
And now I live and now my life is done.

I sought my death and found it in my womb,
I looked for life and saw it was a shade,
I trod the earth and knew it was my tomb,
And now I die, and now I was but made;
My glass is full, and now my glass is run,
And now I live, and now my life is done.

CHIDIOCK TICHBORNE

Nervous Prostration

I MARRIED a man of the Croydon class
When I was twenty-two.
And I vex him, and he bores me
Till we don't know what to do!
It isn't good form in the Croydon class
To say you love your wife,
So I spend my days with the tradesmen's books
And pray for the end of life.

In green fields are blossoming trees
And a golden wealth of gorse,
And young birds sing for joy of worms:
It's perfectly clear, of course,
That it wouldn't be taste in the Croydon class
To sing over dinner or tea:
But I sometimes wish the gentleman
Would turn and talk to me!

But every man of the Croydon class
Lives in terror of joy and speech.
'Words are betrayers,' 'Joys are brief' –
The maxims their wise ones teach –
And for all my labour of love and life
I shall be clothed and fed,
And they'll give me an orderly funeral
When I'm still enough to be dead.

ANNA WICKHAM

They flee from me

THEY flee from me that sometime did me seek
With naked foot stalking in my chamber.
I have seen them gentle, tame, and meek
That now are wild and do not remember
That sometime they put themself in danger
To take bread at my hand; and now they range
Busily seeking with a continual change.

Thanked be fortune it hath been otherwise
Twenty times better, but once in special,
In thin array after a pleasant guise,
When her loose gown from her shoulders did fall
And she me caught in her arms long and small,
Therewithal sweetly did me kiss
And softly said, 'Dear heart, how like you this?'

It was no dream: I lay broad waking:
But all is turned through my gentleness
Into a strange fashion of forsaking.
And I have leave to go of her goodness
And she also to use newfangleness.
But since that I so kindly am served
I would fain know what she hath deserved.

SIR THOMAS WYATT

Babiy Yar

Over Babiy Yar
there are no memorials.
The steep hillside like a rough inscription.
I am frightened.
Today I am as old as the Jewish race.
I seem to myself a Jew at this moment.
I, wandering in Egypt.
I, crucified. I perishing.
Even today the mark of the nails.
I think also of Dreyfus. I am he.
The Philistine my judge and my accuser.
Cut off by bars and cornered,
ringed round, spat at, lied about;
the screaming ladies with the Brussels lace
poke me in the face with parasols.
I am also a boy in Belostok,
the dropping blood spreads across the floor,
the public-bar heroes are rioting
in an equal stench of garlic and of drink.
I have no strength, go spinning from a boot,
shriek useless prayers that they don't listen to;
with a cackle of 'Thrash the kikes and save Russia!'
the corn-chandler is beating up my mother.
I seem to myself like Anna Frank
to be transparent as an April twig
and am in love, I have no need for words,
I need for us to look at one another.
How little we have to see or to smell
separated from foliage and the sky,
how much, how much in the dark room
gently embracing each other.
They're coming. Don't be afraid.
The booming and banging of the spring.
It's coming this way. Come to me.
Quickly, give me your lips.
They're battering in the door. Roar of the ice.

[179]

Over Babiy Yar
rustle of the wild grass.
The trees look threatening, look like judges.
And everything is one silent cry.
Taking my hat off
I feel myself slowly going grey.
And I am one silent cry
over the many thousands of the buried;
am every old man killed here,
every child killed here.
O my Russian people, I know you.
Your nature is international.
Foul hands rattle your clean name.
I know the goodness of my country.
How horrible it is that pompous title
the anti-semites calmly call themselves,
Society of the Russian People.
No part of me can ever forget it.
When the last anti-semite on the earth
is buried for ever
let the International ring out.
No Jewish blood runs among my blood,
but I am as bitterly and hardly hated
by every anti-semite
as if I were a Jew. By this
I am a Russian.

YEVGENY YEVTUSHENKO

THE CONTRIBUTORS

List of Contributors

Numbers indicate the order in which the contributors listed their chosen poems; an asterisk indicates where the contributors specifically put their poems in no order of preference.

Martin Amis
1 Paradise Lost   John Milton
2 To his Coy Mistress   Andrew Marvell
3 Ulysses   Alfred, Lord Tennyson
4 Sailing to Byzantium   W. B. Yeats
5 The Rime of the Ancient   Samuel Taylor Coleridge
  Mariner
6 The Love Song of J. Alfred   T. S. Eliot
  Prufrock
7 'Bright star, would I were   John Keats
  steadfast as thou art'
8 The Sick Rose   William Blake
9 Strange Meeting   Wilfred Owen
10 Exile's Letter   Ezra Pound

Jeffrey Archer
1 The Thousandth Man   Rudyard Kipling
2 Disabled   Wilfred Owen
3 Under Milk Wood   Dylan Thomas
4 The Whitsun Weddings   Philip Larkin
5 'The world's a stage'   Hilaire Belloc
6 The Old Vicarage,   Rupert Brooke
  Grantchester
7 In Westminster Abbey   Sir John Betjeman
8 The Burial of Sir John Moore   Charles Wolfe
  after Corunna
9 Mad Dogs and Englishmen   Noel Coward
10 'How doth the little crocodile'   Lewis Carroll

Pamela Armstrong
* On Monsieur's Departure   Queen Elizabeth I
  'Upon her soothing breast'   Emily Brontë
  Maternity   Alice Meynell

'There was a small woman called G . . .'	Anonymous
Nervous Prostration	Anna Wickham
The Battle Hymn of the Republic	Julia Ward Howe
The Second Wife	Lizette Woodworth Reese
Wild Women Blues	Ida Cox
'I think I was enchanted'	Emily Dickinson
Adam Pos'd	Anne Finch, Countess of Winchilsea

Dame Peggy Ashcroft

★ Ode: Intimations of Immortality	William Wordsworth
Lycidas	John Milton
The Love Song of J. Alfred Prufrock	T. S. Eliot
The Dong with a Luminous Nose	Edward Lear
'The lowest trees have tops'	Sir Edward Dyer
The Ecstasy	John Donne
'Fear no more the heat o' the sun' (*from* Cymbeline, IV.ii)	William Shakespeare
A Toccata of Galuppi's	Robert Browning
I'm Explaining a Few Things	Pablo Neruda
Afterwards	Thomas Hardy

Beryl Bainbridge

1 Non Sum Qualis Eram	Ernest Dowson
2 Dover Beach	Matthew Arnold
3 'So, we'll go no more a roving'	Lord Byron
4 Little Gidding	T. S. Eliot
5 Sun and Fun: Song of a night-club proprietress	Sir John Betjeman
6 The Highwayman	Alfred Noyes
7 The Lady of Shalott	Alfred, Lord Tennyson
8 The Slave's Dream	H. W. Longfellow
9 The Burial of Sir John Moore after Corunna	Charles Wolfe
10 If –	Rudyard Kipling

The Rt Hon Kenneth Baker MP

1	Sonnet 60: 'Like as the waves make towards the pebbled shore'	William Shakespeare
2	The Prologue to the Canterbury Tales	Geoffrey Chaucer
3	L'Allegro	John Milton
4	Bishop Blougram's Apology	Robert Browning
5	Pied Beauty	Gerard Manley Hopkins
6	Tintern Abbey	William Wordsworth
7	The 'Mary Gloster'	Rudyard Kipling
8	The Witsun Weddings	Philip Larkin
9	Little Gidding	T. S. Eliot
10	The Rape of the Lock	Alexander Pope

Richard Baker OBE

1	Ode to a Nightingale	John Keats
2	Sonnet 116: 'Let me not to the marriage of true minds'	William Shakespeare
3	Sonnet 104: 'To me, fair friend, you never can be old'	William Shakespeare
4	Four Quartets	T. S. Eliot
5	Christmas	Sir John Betjeman
6	Spring Offensive	Wilfred Owen
7	The Autumnal	John Donne
8	To his Coy Mistress	Andrew Marvell
9	At a Solemn Music	John Milton
10	'The world is too much with us'	William Wordsworth

Joan Bakewell

★	The Lie	Sir Walter Raleigh
	Portrait of a Lady	T. S. Eliot
	Villanelle	Harry Guest
	To his Coy Mistress	Andrew Marvell
	Sonnet 110: 'Alas, 'tis true, I have gone here and there'	William Shakespeare

'Fear no more the heat o' the   William Shakespeare
    sun' (*from* Cymbeline,
    IV.ii)
Let Me Die a Youngman's   Roger McGough
    Death
Not Waving but Drowning   Stevie Smith
Church Going   Philip Larkin
Remembrance   Emily Brontë

The Rt Hon John Biffen MP
1 'When I was one-and-twenty'   A. E. Housman
    (*from* A Shropshire Lad,
    xiii)
2 The Lost Leader   Robert Browning
3 I. M. – R. T. Hamilton Bruce   W. E. Henley
4 Fire and Ice   Robert Frost
5 To the Virgins, to make much   Robert Herrick
    of Time
6 Anthem for Doomed Youth   Wilfred Owen
7 Le Lac   Alphonse Lamartine
8 To his Coy Mistress   Andrew Marvell
9 Ode: Intimations of   William Wordsworth
    Immortality
10 Autumn   Roy Campbell

Maeve Binchy
1 To Autumn   John Keats
2 Ode to the West Wind   Percy Bysshe Shelley
3 To his Coy Mistress   Andrew Marvell
4 Lays of Ancient Rome   Thomas Babington Macaulay
5 The Song of Hiawatha   H. W. Longfellow
6 L'Allegro   John Milton
7 Il Penseroso   John Milton
8 Tintern Abbey   William Wordsworth
9 My Dark Rosaleen!   J. C. Mangan

Claire Bloom
1 'So, we'll go no more a   Lord Byron
    roving'
2 Ode on Melancholy   John Keats

3	The Windhover	Gerard Manley Hopkins
4	'Because I could not stop for Death'	Emily Dickinson
5	Man and Wife	Robert Lowell
6	East Coker	T. S. Eliot
7	Leda and the Swan	W. B. Yeats
8	The Lotos-Eaters	Alfred, Lord Tennyson
9	To Sleep	John Keats
10	Ode to a Nightingale	John Keats

Richard Briers

1	The Solitary Reaper	William Wordsworth
2	The Whitsun Weddings	Philip Larkin
3	Jabberwocky	Lewis Carroll
4	Albert and the Lion	Marriott Edgar
5	Gus: the Theatre Cat	T. S. Eliot
6	Death in Leamington	Sir John Betjeman
7	'Now the hungry lion roars' (*from* A Midsummer Night's Dream, V.i)	William Shakespeare
8	The Burning of the Leaves	Laurence Binyon
9	Lines in memoriam regarding the entertainment I gave on 31st of March 1893 in Reform Street Hall, Dundee	William McGonagall
10	'I once was out with Henry in the days/When Henry loved me' (*from* Becket, V.ii)	Alfred, Lord Tennyson

Dora Bryan

★	Daffodils	William Wordsworth
	Renouncement	Alice Meynell
	When I'm Alone	Siegfried Sassoon
	The Question	Percy Bysshe Shelley
	The Walrus and the Carpenter	Lewis Carroll
	Cargoes	John Masefield
	If I Should Ever by Chance	Edward Thomas
	Milk for the Cat	Harold Monro
	Leisure	W. H. Davies
	Upon Westminster Bridge	William Wordsworth

James Burke

1	The Relic	John Donne
2	The Collar	George Herbert
3	To his Coy Mistress	Andrew Marvell
4	'They flee from me that sometime did me seek'	Sir Thomas Wyatt
5	La Figlia Che Piange	T. S. Eliot
6	Sonnet 30: 'When to the sessions of sweet silent thought'	William Shakespeare
7	'From far, from eve and morning' (*from* A Shropshire Lad, xxxii)	A. E. Housman
8	The Lake Isle of Innisfree	W. B. Yeats
9	My Last Duchess	Robert Browning
10	When You are Old	W. B. Yeats

Sir Alastair Burnet

1	Dover Beach	Matthew Arnold
2	Sonnet 18: 'Shall I compare thee to a summer's day?'	William Shakespeare
3	Ode: Intimations of Immortality	William Wordsworth
4	Ode on a Grecian Urn	John Keats
5	Eheu, fugaces (To Postumus)	Quintus Horatius Flaccus (Horace)
6	'How do I love thee?' (*from* Sonnets from the Portuguese, xliii)	Elizabeth Barrett Browning
7	A Poor Scholar of the Forties	Padraic Colum
8	Adonais	Percy Bysshe Shelley
9	Under Ben Bulben, vi	W. B. Yeats
10	Timor Mortis Conturbat Me	William Dunbar

John Carey

1	To Autumn	John Keats
2	Lycidas	John Milton
3	'A slumber did my spirit seal'	William Wordsworth

4	Tithonus	Alfred, Lord Tennyson
5	The Love Song of J. Alfred Prufrock	T. S. Eliot
6	Sonnet 71: 'No longer mourn for me when I am dead'	William Shakespeare
7	Sailing to Byzantium	W. B. Yeats
8	A Nocturnal upon St Lucy's Day	John Donne
9	An Arundel Tomb	Philip Larkin
10	Lullaby: 'Lay your sleeping head, my love'	W. H. Auden

Catherine Cookson OBE

1	The Children's Hour	H. W. Longfellow
2	Sonnet 60: 'Like as the waves make towards the pebbled shore'	William Shakespeare
3	The Eve of Waterloo	Lord Byron
4	In the Dordogne	John Peale Bishop
5	Cities and Thrones and Powers	Rudyard Kipling
6	Song: 'Goe, and catche a falling starre'	John Donne
7	Verses Written in a Lady's Sherlock 'Upon Death'	Earl Of Chesterfield
8	An Elegy on a Lap Dog	John Gay
9	'Know then thyself, presume not God to scan' (*from* An Essay on Man, II)	Alexander Pope
10	The Inquest	W. H. Davies

Jilly Cooper

1	The Rime of the Ancient Mariner	Samuel Taylor Coleridge
2	The Flower	George Herbert
3	Tintern Abbey	William Wordsworth
4	To an Adopted Child	Anonymous
5	Stopping by Woods on a Snowy Evening	Robert Frost
6	Horatius	Thomas Babington Macaulay
7	Ulysses	Alfred, Lord Tennyson

8 'Tell me not here, it needs not saying'   A. E. Housman

9 The Galloping Cat   Stevie Smith

10 'Forth goes the woodman, leaving unconcerned/The cheerful haunts of man' (*from* The Task, V)   William Cowper

Cyril Cusack

1 The Leaden Echo and the Golden Echo   Gerard Manley Hopkins

2 Felix Randal   Gerard Manley Hopkins

3 The Windhover   Gerard Manley Hopkins

4 Sonnet 18: 'Shall I compare thee to a summer's day?'   William Shakespeare

5 In Memory of Eva Gore-Booth and Con Markiewicz   W. B. Yeats

6 Upon Westminister Bridge   William Wordsworth

7 A Christmas Childhood   Patrick Kavanagh

8 La Figlia Che Piange   T. S. Eliot

9 Golden Stockings   Oliver St John Gogarty

10 The O'Rahilly   W. B. Yeats

Tessa Dahl

1 When You are Old   W. B. Yeats

2 The Sunlight on the Garden   Louis MacNeice

3 The Busy Heart   Rupert Brooke

4 'The hand that signed the paper felled a city'   Dylan Thomas

5 The Final Word   Dom Moraes

6 Ghosts   Elizabeth Jennings

7 Another Time   W. H. Auden

8 If I should Learn, in Some Quite Casual Way   Edna St Vincent Millay

9 The Donkey   G. K. Chesterton

10 Uphill   Christina Rossetti

Charles Dance

1 Sonnet 29: 'When, in disgrace   William Shakespeare
   with Fortune and men's
   eyes'
2 Kubla Khan   Samuel Taylor Coleridge
3 A Dream in the Luxembourg   Richard Aldington
4 'Do not go gentle into that   Dylan Thomas
   good night'
5 Ballad of the Spanish Civil   Federico García Lorca
   Guard
6 Waiting for the Barbarians   C. P. Cavafy
7 The Vulture   Hilaire Belloc
8 Not Waving but Drowning   Stevie Smith
9 Party Piece   Brian Patten
10 The Aesthete (*from* The Bab   Sir W. S. Gilbert
   Ballads)

Len Deighton

1 The Ballad of Reading Gaol   Oscar Wilde
2 The Hollow Men   T. S. Eliot
3 Exposure   Wilfred Owen
4 Anthem for Doomed Youth   Wilfred Owen
5 Delight in Disorder   Robert Herrick
6 Judging Distances   Henry Reed
7 Harbour Ferry   Roy Fuller
8 Song of the Dying Gunner   Charles Causley
9 Sonnet 29: 'When, in disgrace   William Shakespeare
   with Fortune and men's
   eyes'
10 If –   Rudyard Kipling

Jonathan Dimbleby

1 'Prithee go in thyself' (*from*   William Shakespeare
   King Lear, III.iv)
2 Show Saturday   Philip Larkin
3 On First Looking into   John Keats
   Chapman's Homer
4 Clearances (Sonnet 7)   Seamus Heaney
5 An Arundel Tomb   Philip Larkin
6 Two in the Campagna   Robert Browning
7 East Coker   T. S. Eliot
8 Boy at the Window   Richard Wilbur

| 9 The Hawk in the Rain | Ted Hughes |
| 10 September 1st, 1939 | W. H. Auden |

Frederick Forsyth
1 The Rubáiyát of Omar Khayyám	Edward Fitzgerald
2 The Soldier	Rupert Brooke
3 Ode to a Nightingale	John Keats
4 Elegy Written in a Country Churchyard	Thomas Gray
5 The Ballad of Reading Goal	Oscar Wilde
6 L'Ennui	Charles Baudelaire
7 Sacra Fames	Charles Baudelaire
8 The Burial of Sir John Moore after Corunna	Charles Wolfe
9 The Rime of the Ancient Mariner	Samuel Taylor Coleridge
10 The Revenge, A Ballad of the Fleet	Alfred, Lord Tennyson

Dick Francis
1 Under Milk Wood	Dylan Thomas
2 Jim	Hilaire Belloc
3 The Law the Lawyers Know About	H. D. C. Pepler
4 Song: 'For Mercy, Courage, Kindness, Mirth'	Laurence Binyon
5 If –	Rudyard Kipling
6 How they brought the Good News from Ghent to Aix	Robert Browning
7 'Do not go gentle into that good night'	Dylan Thomas

George MacDonald Fraser
★ 'When icicles hang by the wall' (*from* Love's Labour's Lost, V.i)	William Shakespeare
'My love is like a red, red rose'	Robert Burns
The Listeners	Walker de la Mare
The Crowning of Dreaming John	John Drinkwater

The Golden Journey to Samarkand	J. E. Flecker
I Remember, I Remember	Thomas Hood
The Choice	Dante Gabriel Rossetti
The Ballad of East and West	Rudyard Kipling
Captain Stratton's Fancy	John Masefield
The Rolling English Road	G. K. Chesterton

Fiona Fullerton

1. 'How do I love thee?' (*from* Sonnets from the Portuguese, xliii) — Elizabeth Barrett Browning
2. Halfway Down — A. A. Milne
3. Vespers — A. A. Milne
4. A Thought — A. A. Milne
5. If – — Rudyard Kipling
6. Daffodils — William Wordsworth
7. Morte d'Arthur — Alfred, Lord Tennyson
8. The Walrus and the Carpenter — Lewis Carroll
9. The Pied Piper of Hamelin — Robert Browning
10. The Rime of the Ancient Mariner — Samuel Taylor Coleridge

Liza Goddard

1. The Pasture — Robert Frost
2. The Road not Taken — Robert Frost
3. Hunter Trials — Sir John Betjeman
4. To his Coy Mistress — Andrew Marvell
5. Maud — Alfred, Lord Tennyson
6. Love's Growth — John Donne
7. Lullaby: 'Lay your sleeping head, my love' — W. H. Auden
8. Death of an Actor — Hugo Williams
9. An Ode to the Queen on Her Jubilee Year — William McGonagall
10. Matilda — Hilaire Belloc

The Rt Hon Bryan Gould MP

1. On his Blindness — John Milton
2. Ozymandias — Percy Bysshe Shelley
3. To his Coy Mistress — Andrew Marvell

4	Porphyria's Lover	Robert Browning
5	The Donkey	G. K. Chesterton
6	The Tiger	William Blake
7	Sonnet 18: 'Shall I compare thee to a summer's day?'	William Shakespeare
8	On First Looking into Chapman's Homer	John Keats
9	Oxford: Sudden Illness at the Bus-stop	Sir John Betjeman
10	'My love is like a red, red rose'	Robert Burns

Mike Harding

1	Pied Beauty	Gerard Manley Hopkins
2	The Love Song of J. Alfred Prufrock	T. S. Eliot
3	Exposure	Wilfred Owen
4	The Whitsun Weddings	Philip Larkin
5	North	Seamus Heaney
6	Victor Jara of Chile	Adrian Mitchell
7	The Sun Rising	John Donne
8	'And death shall have no dominion'	Dylan Thomas
9	The Emperor of Ice-Cream	Wallace Stevens
10	Lady Lazarus	Sylvia Plath

The Rt Hon Roy Hattersley MP

1	Dover Beach	Matthew Arnold
2	Sonnet 18: 'Shall I compare thee to a summer's day?'	William Shakespeare
3	Sonnet 29: 'When, in disgrace with Fortune and men's eyes'	William Shakespeare
4	Naming of Parts	Henry Reed
5	A Shropshire Lad	A. E. Housman
6	American Names	Stephen Vincent Benét
7	One Word More	Robert Browning
8	Dockery and Son	Philip Larkin
9	In Memory of Eva Gore-Booth and Con Markiewicz	W. B. Yeats
10	Lycidas	John Milton

Nigel Hawthorne

★	I Remember, I Remember	Philip Larkin
	Sonnet 116: 'Let me not to the marriage of true minds'	William Shakespeare
	Journey of the Magi	T. S. Eliot
	Slough	Sir John Betjeman
	Babi Yar	Yevgeny Yevtushenko
	Coming Round	Christopher Hope
	The Night Mail	W. H. Auden
	The Rime of the Ancient Mariner	Samuel Taylor Coleridge
	Attack	Siegfried Sassoon
	Home Thoughts, from Abroad	Robert Browning

The Rt Hon Denis Healey CH MBE MP

1	Sonnet 73: 'That time of year thou mayst in me behold'	William Shakespeare
2	The Second Coming	W. B. Yeats
3	Fern Hill	Dylan Thomas
4	'At the round earths imagined corners'	John Donne
5	Ode to a Nightingale	John Keats
6	'So, we'll go no more a roving'	Lord Byron
7	'Thou art indeed just, Lord'	Gerard Manley Hopkins
8	The Antiplatonick	John Cleveland
9	Burnt Norton	T. S. Eliot
10	Lullaby: 'Lay your sleeping head, my love'	W. H. Auden

James Herriot OBE

1	Ozymandias	Percy Bysshe Shelley
2	Ode to a Nightingale	John Keats
3	Ode: Intimations of Immortality	William Wordsworth
4	The Old Vicarage, Grantchester	Rupert Brooke
5	The Garden of Proserpine	Algernon Charles Swinburne
6	Invictus	W. E. Henley
7	Epitaph on an Army of Mercenaries	A. E. Housman

8 The Lake Isle of Innisfree	W. B. Yeats
9 Adlestrop	Edward Thomas
10 'My love is like a red, red rose'	Robert Burns

Sir Michael Hordern

1 'Our revels now are ended' (*from* The Tempest, IV.i)	William Shakespeare
2 'The world is too much with us'	William Wordsworth
3 Inversnaid	Gerard Manley Hopkins
4 La Belle Dame sans Merci	John Keats
5 An Epitaph: 'Here lies a most beautiful lady'	Walter de la Mare
6 Jim	Hilaire Belloc
7 At Castle Boterel	Thomas Hardy
8 Adlestrop	Edward Thomas
9 Tarantella	Hilaire Belloc
10 Prayer before Birth	Louis MacNeice

Barry Humphries

1 Here Live Your Life Out!	Robert Graves
2 Moonlit Apples	John Drinkwater
3 To My Daughter	Stephen Spender
4 The Way through the Woods	Rudyard Kipling
5 Piano	D. H. Lawrence
6 Love and the Child	Ruth Pitter
7 Envoi	Anna Wickham

Felicity Kendal

★ A Considered Reply to a Child	Jonathan Price
To his Coy Mistress	Andrew Marvell
it may not always be so	e. e. cummings
The Definition of Love	Andrew Marvell
A Pity. We Were Such a Good Invention	Yehuda Amichai
The Good-Morrow	John Donne
My Lover	Wendy Cope
Remembrance	Sir Thomas Wyatt

Sonnet 18: 'Shall I compare thee to a summer's day?'	William Shakespeare
The Song of Wandering Ængus	W. B. Yeats

Glenys Kinnock
1	Strange Meeting	Wilfred Owen
2	The child is not dead	Ingrid Jonker
3	Sonnet 29: 'When, in disgrace with Fortune and men's eyes'	William Shakespeare
4	A Grammarian's Funeral	Robert Browning
5	'There is a nobler glory' (*from* Queen Mab, V)	Percy Bysshe Shelley
6	'Do not go gentle into that good night'	Dylan Thomas
7	The River God of the River Mimram in Hertfordshire	Stevie Smith
8	The Great Tablecloth	Pablo Neruda
9	Reading Scheme	Wendy Cope
10	Land of my Mothers	Idris Davies

Sue Lawley
1	Dover Beach	Matthew Arnold
2	The Love Song of J. Alfred Prufrock	T. S. Eliot
3	To Autumn	John Keats
4	Danny Deever	Rudyard Kipling
5	The Good-Morrow	John Donne
6	The Parting	Michael Drayton
7	The Listeners	Walter de la Mare
8	Home Thoughts, from Abroad	Robert Browning
9	Ozymandias	Percy Bysshe Shelley
10	Morte d'Arthur	Alfred, Lord Tennyson

Elizabeth Longford
1	Sonnet 60: 'Like as the waves make towards the pebbled shore'	William Shakespeare
2	Don Juan	Lord Byron

3	Ode to a Nightingale	John Keats
4	Prometheus Unbound	Percy Bysshe Shelley
5	Purgatorio	Dante Alighieri
6	Tiresias	Alfred, Lord Tennyson
7	The Second Coming	W. B. Yeats
8	'To be a pilgrim'	John Bunyan
9	Tintern Abbey	William Wordsworth
10	'Death be not proud, though some have called thee'	John Donne

Ian McKellen

★	The Leaden Echo and the Golden Echo	Gerard Manley Hopkins
	The Ballad of Reading Gaol	Oscar Wilde
	To his Coy Mistress	Andrew Marvell
	An Irish Airman Foresees his Death	W. B. Yeats
	In my Craft or Sullen Art	Dylan Thomas
	Piano	D. H. Lawrence
	Anthem for Doomed Youth	Wilfred Owen
	The Prelude, Book II	William Wordsworth
	Sonnet 20: 'A woman's face with Nature's own hand painted'	William Shakespeare

Anna Massey

1	Sonnet 18: 'Shall I compare thee to a summer's day'	William Shakespeare
2	Sonnet 66: 'Tired with all these, for restful death I cry'	William Shakespeare
3	He Wishes for the Cloths of Heaven	W. B. Yeats
4	The Song of Wandering Ængus	W. B. Yeats
5	The Soldier	Rupert Brooke
6	To Autumn	John Keats
7	On his Blindness	John Milton
8	Delight in Disorder	Robert Herrick
9	Sonnet 12: 'When I do count the clock that tells the time'	William Shakespeare

3 The Funeral of Youth: Rupert Brooke
  Threnody
4 Indoor Games near Newbury   Sir John Betjeman
5 The Garden   Harold Monro
6 The Old Vicarage,   Rupert Brooke
  Grantchester
7 Tangerines   Hugo Williams
8 The Waste Land   T. S. Eliot
9 Oxford   Tom Lovatt-Williams
10 L'Envoie   Hilaire Belloc

Beryl Reid
  1 'How do I love thee?' (*from*   Elizabeth Barrett Browning
    Sonnets from the
    Portuguese, xliii)
  2 Solitude   A. A. Milne
  3 'My love is like a red, red Robert Burns
    rose'
  4 King John's Christmas   A. A. Milne
  5 Daffodils   William Wordsworth
  6 Christmas Day   Spike Milligan
  7 'Now sleeps the crimson   Alfred, Lord Tennyson
    petal, now the white' (*from*
    The Princess, VII)
  8 A Fond Kiss   Robert Burns
  9 The Bells of Heaven   Ralph Hodgson
 10 The Friend   A. A. Milne

Jack Rosenthal
  1 Psalm 23   Authorised Version of the Bible
  2 To his Coy Mistress   Andrew Marvell
  3 'Tomorrow, and tomorrow,   William Shakespeare
    and tomorrow' (*from*
    Macbeth, V.v)
  4 Dulce Et Decorum Est   Wilfred Owen
  5 The Love Song of J. Alfred T. S. Eliot
    Prufrock
  6 Easter 1916   W. B. Yeats
  7 Frank Mills (*from* the musical Jerome Ragni and James Rado
    Hair)
  8 The Rime of the Ancient   Samuel Taylor Coleridge
    Mariner

| 9 | London | William Blake |
| 10 | The Song of Hiawatha | H. W. Longfellow |

Nick Ross

1	Sunlight	Seamus Heaney
2	When You are Old	W. B. Yeats
3	He Wishes for the Cloths of Heaven	W. B. Yeats
4	'Dear Bankers, pay the undermentioned hounds'	A. P. Herbert
5	'Dear Sir, it is with pleasure that I thank'	A. L. Grove
6	The Love Song of J. Alfred Prufrock	T.S. Eliot
7	Parliament Hill Fields	Sir John Betjeman
8	Naming of Parts	Henry Reed
9	Annus Mirabilis	Philip Larkin
10	Matilda	Hilaire Belloc

Sir Peter Scott CH CBE DSC FRS

1	The Hunting of the Snark	Lewis Carroll
2	Sonnet 30: 'When to the sessions of sweet silent thought'	William Shakespeare
3	To Autumn	John Keats
4	Skimbleshanks: the Railway Cat	T. S. Eliot
5	Christmas	E. Hilton Young
6	The Knight Whose Armour didn't Squeak	A. A. Milne
7	The Revenge, A Ballad of the Fleet	Alfred, Lord Tennyson
8	To a Skylark	Percy Bysshe Shelley
9	In the Public Gardens	Sir John Betjeman
10	Ducks	F. W. Harvey

The Rt Hon David Steel MP

1	Holy Willie's Prayer	Robert Burns
2	'And death shall have no dominion'	Dylan Thomas
3	Dulce Et Decorum Est	Wilfred Owen

4 The Eve of St Agnes   John Keats
5 'So, we'll go no more a   Lord Byron
    roving'
6 Embro to the Ploy   Robert Garrick
7 Trench Duty   Siegfried Sassoon
8 Tam o'Shanter   Robert Burns
9 'Bright be the place in thy   Lord Byron
    soul'
10 Man was made to Mourn   Robert Burns

Dorothy Tutin
1 'Fear no more the heat o' the   William Shakespeare
    sun' (*from* Cymbeline,
    IV.ii)
2 Sonnet 29: 'When, in disgrace   William Shakespeare
    with Fortune and men's
    eyes'
3 'O mistress mine, where are   William Shakespeare
    you roaming' (*from*
    Twelfth Night, II.iii)
4 Ode to a Nightingale   John Keats
5 'When I have fears that I may   John Keats
    cease to be'
6 'The splendour falls on castle   Alfred, Lord Tennyson
    walls' (*from* The Princess,
    IV)
7 'Now sleeps the crimson petal,   Alfred, Lord Tennyson
    now the white' (*from* The
    Princess, VII)
8 I Am   John Clare
9 'And now I live and now I   Chidiock Tichborne
    die'
10 'Now dawns the invisible'   Emily Brontë

Katharine Whitehorn
1 Sonnet 73: 'That time of year   William Shakespeare
    thou mayst in me behold'
2 A Valediction: forbidding   John Donne
    mourning
3 Paradise Lost   John Milton
4 Ode: Intimations of   William Wordsworth
    Immortality

5	Dover Beach	Matthew Arnold
6	Andrea del Sarto	Robert Browning
7	Anthem for Doomed Youth	Wilfred Owen
8	The Map of Verona	Henry Reed
9	The First of May	A. E. Housman
10	The Second Coming	W. B. Yeats

Note: Katherine Whitehorn's list is not of her favourite poems, but of some of the poems that have meant most to her.

Index of Poets

Index of First Lines

[205]

Lars Porsena of Clusium 95
Let me die a youngman's death 165
Let us begin and carry up this corpse 67
Little Boy kneels at the foot of the bed 51

Matilda told such Dreadful Lies 16
Mine eyes have seen the glory of the coming of the Lord 158
My Love is of a birth as rare 163
My prime of youth is but a frost of cares 176

No more wine? then we'll push back chairs and talk 65
No, No! go not to Lethe, neither twist 21
Not flesh of my flesh 58
Now that we'e done our best and worst, and parted 41

O what can ail thee, knight-at-arms 88
O wild West Wind, thou breath of Autumn's being 30
One wept whose only child was dead 166
Out of the night that covers me 47
Over Babiy Yar 179

Prometheus Monarch of Gods and Daemons, and all Spirits 105

Quinquereme of Nineveh from distant Ophir 164

St Agnes' Eve – Ah, bitter chill it was! 90
Seven days he travelled 144
She knows, being woman, that for him she holds 172
She taught me what her uncle once taught her 85
Since I was ten I have not been unkind 129
Some say the world will end in fire 80

Tamed by *Miltown*, we lie on Mother's bed 122
The child is not dead 20
The *Curfeu* tolls the Knell of parting Day 81
The day that *Youth* had died 42
The hand that signed the paper felled a city 109
The horses are black 118
The law the lawyers know about 52
The rain set early in tonight 71
The sunlight on the garden 24
The woods decay, the woods decay and fall 107
There are plenty of people to despise the dreamer of day-dreams 35
There was a small woman called G 132
There was a sound of revelry by night 44
There was a sunlit absence 18
There's a famous seaside place called Blackpool 75
There's a whisper down the line at 11.39 78
They amputated 131
They flee from me that sometime me did seek 178

Acknowledgements

Every effort has been made to trace copyright holders but the publishers will be happy to rectify any omissions in future editions. For permission to reprint certain poems in this anthology, acknowledgement is made to the following:

The estate of Richard Aldington for Richard Aldington's 'A Dream in Luxembourg', published by Chatto & Windus; Yehuda Amichai's 'A Pity. We Were Such A Good Invention' by permission of Yehuda Amichai; W.H. Auden's 'Night Mail' reprinted by permission of Faber and Faber Ltd from *Collected Poems* by W.H. Auden edited by Edward Mendelson; Hilaire Belloc's 'Matilda' reprinted by permission of the Peters, Fraser & Dunlop Group Ltd from *Complete Verse*; John Betjeman's 'Hunter Trials' and 'Indoor Games near Newbury' from John Betjeman's *Collected Poems*, John Murray (Publishers) Ltd.; Laurence Binyon's 'For Mercy, Courage, Kindness, Mirth' by permission of Mrs Nicolete Gray and the Society of Authors, on behalf of the Laurence Binyon Estate; Wendy Cope's 'My Lover' reprinted by permission of Faber and Faber Ltd from *Making Cocoa for Kingsley Amis*; E.E. Cummings' 'it may not always be so;and i say' is reprinted from *Complete Poems 1904–1962*, by E.E. Cummings, edited by George J. Firmage, by permission of W.W. Norton & Company Ltd. Copyright © 1923, 1951, 1976, 1991 by the Trustees for the E.E. Cummings Trust and George James Firmage; Walter de la Mare's 'An Epitaph – Here lies a most